FOREWORD by KEVIN GARNETT    AFTERWORD by KARL MALONE

# AT THE BUZZER!

## Havlicek steals, Erving soars, Magic deals, Michael scores
## THE GREATEST MOMENTS IN NBA HISTORY

By Bryan Burwell    Narration by Bill Walton

DOUBLEDAY

NEW YORK — LONDON — TORONTO — SYDNEY — AUCKLAND

# CREDITS

## AT THE BUZZER!

Published by Doubleday, a division of Random House, Inc.
1540 Broadway, New York, NY 10036

Doubleday and the portrayal of an anchor with a dolphin are trademarks of Doubleday, a division of Random House, Inc.

Library of Congress Cataloging-in-Publication Data is available from the Publisher.

ISBN 0-385-50145-5

Printed in Barcelona, Spain

First Edition

October 2001

1 2 3 4 5 6 7 8 9 10

## Designed and Produced by:

**Rare Air Media**
1711 N. Paulina, Suite 311
Chicago, IL 60622

## Text by:

BRYAN BURWELL, an award-winning sports journalist for HBO Sports, covered his first pro basketball game — New York Nets versus Virginia Squires — as a college freshman in 1974. A veteran reporter and commentator for more than two decades, Burwell writes monthly columns for *Hoop* magazine and the *Sports Business Journal*, and has worked for Turner Sports, and *USA Today*. Burwell is the first back-to-back winner of the National Association of Black Journalists' award for sports writing and was named one of the top five columnists in the country by the Associated Press Sports Editors in 1989. He lives in Virginia with his wife, Dawnn, and daughter Victoria.

## Narration by:

BILL WALTON, one of the 50 Greatest Players in NBA History, currently serves as an analyst for NBC's coverage of the NBA. A three-time NCAA Player of the Year, Walton was a member of UCLA's undefeated NCAA championship teams in 1972 and 1973, a team that won an unprecedented 88 straight games, and was the first overall pick of the 1974 NBA Draft. The 6-foot-11 Hall of Famer helped the Portland Trail Blazers win the NBA title in 1977 and also was on the Boston Celtics championship squad in 1986. In addition to his work at NBC, Walton provides commentary on Los Angeles Clippers telecasts as well as analysis on Turner Sports' NBA coverage. He lives in San Diego with his wife Lori and is the proud father of four sons, Adam, Nate, Luke and Chris.

## PHOTOGRAPHY CREDITS

| | | | |
|---|---|---|---|
| RAY AMATI | 112 | DALLAS MAVERICKS PR DEPT. | 169 |
| AP WIDE WORLD PHOTO | 51, 84, 86, 142, 143, 152, 153, 172, 173, 174, 174, 175 | GARY DINEEN | 157 |
| BILL BAPTIST | 32, 33, 35, 106, 115, 128 | GARRETT ELLWOOD | 161 |
| JOHN BAZEMORE/ AP WIDE WORLD PHOTO | 198 | ED FITZGERALD | 144 |
| RANDY BELICE | 186 | SAM FORENCICH | 46, 161 |
| LAWRENCE BERMAN | 106, 188 | GREG FOSTER | 200 |
| ANDREW D. BERNSTEIN | 22, 26, 29, 46, 48, 52, 53, 60-61, 73, 74, 75, 102, 103, 122, 123, 129, 140, 141, 148, 149, 150, 151, 153, 155, 157, 176, 177, 204, 208, 211, 212, 215, 216 | GEORGE FREY | 178 |
| | | JESSE GARRABRANT | 9, 29, 70 |
| | | GLOBE PHOTOS, INC. | 49, 66, 143, 168 |
| | | BARRY GOSSAGE | 160, 187 |
| | | RUSS HALFORD/ SPORTS ILLUSTRATED | 97 |
| NATHANIEL S. BUTLER | 20-21, 30-31, 34-35, 46, 47, 54, 115, 134, 135, 137, 138, 146, 147, 150, 157, 161, 186, 187, 210, 211 | PAT HAMILTON/ SAN ANTONIO EXPRESS-NEWS | 163 |
| | | COURTESY OF JERRY HARKNESS | 24 |
| | | GARY HARWOOD | 44, 45 |
| CAMERA ASSOCIATES | 155 | ANDY HAYT | 72, 117, 179-181, 187 |
| LOU CAPOZZOLA | 197, 208 | JON HAYT | 101 |
| CHICAGO BULLS PR DEPT. | 159 | *HOOP* MAGAZINE/ MALCOM FARLEY | 10 |
| RICHARD CLARKSON/ SPORTS ILLUSTRATED | 193, 194, 195 | WALTER IOOSS, JR./ SPORTS ILLUSTRATED | 133, 136, 170, 201 |
| CORBIS | 51, 121 | WALTER IOOSS, JR. | 96, 105, 156, 159 |
| JIM CUMMINS | 56, 57, 58, 59, 91, 92 | CARL IWASKI | 136 |
| SCOTT CUNNINGHAM | 104, 155, 187, 199 | | |

| | | | |
|---|---|---|---|
| GLENN JAMES | 28, 32, 33, 161, 187 | NBA ENTERTAINMENT | 14, 15, 16, 17, 18, 19, 36, 37, 43, 44, 45, 52, 102, 166, 167, 190, 191 |
| ATIBA JEFFERSON | 8 | | |
| BUD JONES | 25 | NBA PHOTO LIBRARY | 38, 39, 77, 79, 93, 107, 134, 154, 155, 157, 158, 159, 202, 203, 205 |
| FROM THE LENS OF GEORGE KALINSKY, MAJOR LEAGUE GRAPHICS | 108, 109, 113, 139, 182-183, 184, 185 | | |
| | | ANTHONY NESTE | 156, 159 |
| HEINZ KLUETMEIER/ SPORTS ILLUSTRATED | 134 | DICK RAPHAEL/ SPORTS ILLUSTRATED | 77, 78, 79 |
| NEIL LEIFER | 159 | DICK RAPHAEL | 50, 91, 92, 93, 95, 156, 189 |
| ROBERT LEWIS | 159 | | |
| STEVE LIPOFSKY | 80, 82, 190 | KEN REGAN | 90, 92, 110 |
| STEVE LUNDY | 186 | MARC SEROTA | 214 |
| LOS ANGELES TIMES PHOTO | 195 | GREG SHAMUS | 161 |
| LENNOX MCLENDON | 62, 63 | SHEEDY & LONG/ SPORTS ILLUSTRATED | 97 |
| FERNANDO MEDINA | 23, 40, 98-101, 156, 196, 216 | DAVID SHERMAN | 9 |
| DARREN McNAMARA/ ALLSPORT | 130 | CARL SKALAK/ SPORTS ILLUSTRATED | 85, 118 |
| MANNY MILAN/ SPORTS ILLUSTRATED | 2, 42, 76, 77, 192 | NOREN TROTMAN | 112, 114, 116, 207 |
| JOHN W. McDONOUGH/ SPORTS ILLUSTRATED | 81, 83 | PAUL VATHIS | 125, 127 |
| PETER READ MILLER | 213 | JERRY WACHTER | 117, 128, 188 |
| PORTLAND TRAIL BLAZERS PR DEPT. | 87, 88, 89-80 | ROCKY WIDNER | 11, 161 |
| LAYNE MURDOCH | 161 | COURTESY OF WAYNE WITT | 66, 67 |
| | | STEVE WOLTMAN | 46, 187 |

# ACKNOWLEDGMENTS

**The gratitude for this labor of love goes to a multitude of folks:**

*The NBA Editorial gang: Jan Hubbard, a good man, a fine friend, and a writer's editor; John Hareas, my right hand on this project. Whenever I asked, he responded; John Gardella, my sixth man, for the endless research, interviews, writing and fact checking; fact-checkers/proofreaders Jeanne Tang, Barry Rubinstein, Rita Sullivan, Rob Reheuser and Jordan Brenner, for the difficult job of making me look good; and to April Bulger, the heartbeat of the whole operation.*

**The Burwell gang:**

*I thank my wife, Dawnn, for her support and tolerance of my quirky, 24-hour writer's clock. To daughter, Victoria, my gratitude for her inspirational personality. To my parents, Harold and Ursula Burwell, who provided me with the essential tools of the trade — a love of sports (Dad) and an appreciation of the English language (Mom). Thanks to Honey, my aging golden retriever, for her endless companionship on all those early mornings and late evenings.*

*But mostly, to NBA players past and present: their athletic genius was the source of my inspiration. What a wonderful life I live. Someone just paid me to spend the past few months of my existence watching endless tapes of classic hoop videos, and then let me write about it.*

**BRYAN BURWELL**

*Championships and producing stellar book projects are not realized without the commitment and special talent of individuals who put it all on the line in reaching for the ultimate end result. My sincere thanks and appreciation goes to those who took this journey through NBA history with me and made it a better than perfect experience.*

*I would like to thank John Hareas, Jan Hubbard, Brian McIntyre, Terry Lyons and Seth Sylvan of the NBA Sports Communications Group who deserve particular recognition and praise for their friendship, dedication, sacrifice and commitment. I would especially like to thank the thousands of PR people over the 55-year history of the NBA for bringing our heroes to life and most importantly, the NBA players, guys who have made something out of their lives, often coming from the humblest of backgrounds; Guys who represent the hope, the optimism and the positive spirit that make the NBA the world's greatest game.*

*I also would like to thank Jim Podhoretz, Charlie Rosenzweig, Michael Levine and Jonathan Hock of NBA Entertainment. And a big thank you to all of my coaches who have played, all along the way, a major role in shaping me as a person and as a player. And for my own Hall of Fame team, my wife Lori and four sons, Adam, Nate, Luke and Chris for their love, patience and tolerance.*

**BILL WALTON**

---

## SPECIAL THANKS

**At Doubleday:** *Michael Palgon and Peter Gethers.*

**At the NBA:** *David Stern, Russ Granik, Brian McIntyre, Terry Lyons, Mike Bantom, Rory Sparrow, Zelda Spoelstra, William Koenig, Michelle Leftwich, Ayala Deutsch, Victoria Picca and Yvette Chavis.*

**At NBA Entertainment:** *Adam Silver, Gregg Winik, Heidi Ueberroth, Charles Rosenzweig, Michael Levine, Jim Podhoretz, Jonathan Hock, Todd Caso, Chris Weber, Steve Weintraub, Dave Thomas, Andrew Bennett, Trevor Schmidt, Dan Apallo and Tara Russo.*

**At NBA Entertainment Photos:** *Carmin Romanelli, Joe Amati, Dave Bonilla, Scott Yurdin, Mike Klein, John Kristofick, Bennett Renda and all of the sensational photographers listed on the previous page.*

**At Quebecor World:** *Lou Berceli and Bernart Peypoch.*

**At Rare Air Media:** *Mark Vancil, Frank Fochetta, John Vieceli, Andy Pipitone, Dennis Carlson, Melinda Fry, Steve Polacek, Nick LoBue, Nick De Carlo and Shannon Mounts.*

**At Professional Graphics:** *Vince Llamzon, Pete Knipschield, Stan Reynolds, Harold, Dave, Steve and Pat Goley.*

**Also:** *Karl Malone, Kevin Garnett, Michael Jordan, George Gervin, David Thompson, John Havlicek, Bob Lanier, Mel Daniels, Jerry Harkness, Danny Ainge, Danny Manning, Dolph Schayes, Larry Miller, Jim Spanarkel, Jamaal Wilkes, Cliff Puchalski, George Kalinsky, Kevin Sullivan, Harvey Pollack, Dick Motta, Dave Fredman, Wayne Witt, David Allred, Cindy Edman, Tim Frank, John Fawaz, Dennis D'Agostino, Raymond Ridder, Jeff Twiss, Charles Cyr, Tom James and Chuck Stewart.*

# GREATEST

# FOREWORD
by KEVIN GARNETT

*Any book of memorable moments has got to begin with Michael Jordan and The Shot in Cleveland.*

*Well … it doesn't have to be the first moment in this book, but, for 12-year-old*

*Kevin Garnett in Mauldin, S. C.,*

## THAT SHOT WAS THE MOMENT.

I was just starting to play basketball in 1989. I was young and full of enthusiasm. Of course, I'm still full of enthusiasm because every moment that I'm on the basketball court is a great moment for me. At that time, however, I didn't really know anything about the game. I was starting fresh. After watching Michael jump over Craig Ehlo, make that shot and win that game, my life changed. Basketball became my world. It meant everything to me.

And, man, could 12-year-old Kevin Garnett do a sweet Michael Jordan imitation. I actually studied that shot, watched the way he kicked his legs when he released the ball, and flicked his wrists. That inspired me. So I went right outside and started kicking *my* legs, flicking *my* wrist and celebrating.

I found out that it was a lot harder than it looked.

But it was fun. And so pure. Michael's shot gave me hope. I think it gave a lot of kids hope. The hope was that they could someday win a game with a last-second shot, too.

Great moments define the game of basketball. They are basketball at its very best. As you will see in this book, all of the defining moments — except for a few of the memorably funny ones — occur at crucial times. That's because a critical moment puts a player in what looks like an impossible situation, and then demands: "O.K. Can you handle this one? This one needs to be done, or these are the consequences: We lose."

If the shot is missed, you never hear about it. If Magic Johnson doesn't make the junior, junior skyhook in 1987, we all would be thinking about some other things that happened in that series. Same with Michael against Cleveland.

**But those guys made the shots. Great moments are not about the sense of urgency, they're about coming through a situation with a sense of elegance in a time of need. Such moments are like supernovas, so bright that you can see them as clearly as you can see the sun.**

I'm only 25 years old, but I know my great moments. When basketball became my life, it was much more than simply playing. I became a student of the game and a historian. Wilt Chamberlain scored 100 points in a game 14 years before I was born, but I know all about it. Jerry West made the half-court shot against the Knicks six years before I was born, but I've watched the tape and I know all about it. (Do you remember? The game went into overtime and the

Lakers lost.) And it was that same series when Willis Reed gave everybody goose bumps by coming out of the locker room on a bum leg, motivating his teammates to go to their limits and beat the Lakers for the title.

**Man, it is going to be great for everyone to see those moments in this book. And I can't wait to listen to the CDs. They have the** real play-by-play and all-new commentary **that match up with the moments that are listed in the book, and my man Bill Walton is doing the narrating.** Old Bill was one of the greatest centers ever, but have you seen those wild old pictures? He had that frizzy, long red hair with headbands and stuff. Now look at him. All straight, proper and clean cut. But I will tell you, Bill's commentary can sometimes be as wicked as his outlet passes used to be.

In 1997, I made my first All-Star team and, as a basketball historian, nothing could have been more perfect. The NBA was honoring the 50 greatest players, and all the legends were there.

I remember seeing Wilt for the first time. I felt like that 12-year-old kid again. It was like seeing the ultimate basketball god. (No offense MJ, but I got to play against you.) I was hesitant at first. I felt like it was going to be my only chance to say hello, but I had to break through all the security and stuff. I finally told Wilt it was a pleasure to meet him, and he gave me one of the greatest compliments that I could have received from anyone. **He said that he enjoyed watching me play, and told me never to lose the enthusiasm that I have for the game. I promised I wouldn't.**

Wilt Chamberlain! It doesn't get any better than that.

Wilt deserves to be called a basketball god because scoring 100 points in a game is unbelievable. Some teams don't even score 100 points as a team, and that's with five shooters, five good players, on the floor. That tells you a lot about what Wilt did. It says a lot about his professionalism, his drive, his inner strength and his game.

At the 1997 All-Star Game, the legends were everywhere. I saw Dr. J in the elevator, going to the bus. I was on the same floor with Michael in the game. Magic Johnson, Larry Bird, George Mikan (yes, I know George, even though he retired 20 years before I was born), Bill Russell, Kareem Abdul-Jabbar. It was amazing.

**Those are the guys I look up to, because those are the guys who created the moments that inspired me. My generation will be creating many moments for the future, but it's going to be a little tougher for us, and not for the reason you might expect. Many years ago, when great moments occurred, it was almost like, "Wow! Did you see that?" Great athletic moves weren't as com-**

mon as they are today.

Now, we have great athletes making great moves every night. More is expected of us. As a result, we have added a new flavor to the game. I would definitely say the game has gotten more creative, more artistic, and has more flair. That's not to say anything before us was not as good, but we are at a different level.

We have some guys who have already taken things to a new dimension. I thought Vince Carter was incredible in the 2000 dunk contest at Oakland, but did you see him in the Olympics? I did. I was right there when he jumped over a 7-foot-2 guy from France. Check my face when you get to that moment. I don't think even Vince believed it.

I believe we are going to extend the legacy. This young group of players is going to leave you with a lot of memorable moments. But, in the meantime, I think I'll kick back, enjoy the past and listen to the CDs. **I respect the old players and I am honored to be able to follow in their footsteps.** I have a great appreciation for what they accomplished, and I am going to cherish every moment in this book.

1987 NBA Finals, Game 4
[ LOS ANGELES LAKERS 107, BOSTON CELTICS 106 ]
*JUNE 9, 1987*

# CHAPTER 1
# GREAT SHOTS

# THIS MAGIC MOMENT

**When cracking open the vault of the NBA's most memorable moments,
there is nothing more profound than a great shot
*At The Buzzer.***
**Whether it is the sweet sound of a game-winning jumper, the jaw-dropping surprise
of a buzzer-beating heave, or an outrageous fit of staggering athletic inspiration, a great shot is like
some sparkling diamond solitaire. Its brilliance stands alone.**

**With these precious jewels of the game — such as the sight of Magic Johnson gliding across the paint
in the Boston Garden with his dramatic junior, junior skyhook to defeat the Celtics in the 1987
NBA Finals — winning is not a necessity, though it certainly helps. All that is required is the requisite
drama: a rags-to-riches tale; a moment of desperation; a simple twist of fate; or the element of surprise.**

**With all of these great shots, it is the memory of the single moment —
not the final score — that will last for eternity.**

# MAGIC'S ULTIMATE FIRST GAME

**LOS ANGELES LAKERS 103, SAN DIEGO CLIPPERS 102**
*OCTOBER 12, 1979*

It took all of one game for Earvin "Magic" Johnson to symbolize
the purity of competition in the NBA. Great moments are
sometimes mistakenly confused with significant moments.
The notion is that something grand has to be at stake, such as a title
or a record, to elevate the achievement. Johnson was a joyous,
unselfish, tenacious competitor. His brilliance was evident in many
playoff and championship games. But the fact that one remarkable
moment occurred in a seemingly meaningless regular-season game
is a tribute to the greatness Magic brought to the court.

# NO CHAMPIONSHIP; JUST VICTORY

In the 1979-80 season opener between the Los Angeles Lakers and San Diego Clippers, Kareem Abdul-Jabbar scored the winning basket on a breathtaking 18-foot sky-hook at the buzzer, giving the Lakers a 103-102 victory. For Johnson, it was not much different than the last meaningful game he had played in about seven months earlier when his Michigan State team won the NCAA championship. He knew nothing of the way some thought he was supposed to act in the NBA, nothing about being an ultra-cool, detached professional. He knew nothing about the grind of a marathon 82-game season. He knew only that it was a game, a competition, and he wanted to win.

**"Sky-hook, up — and in!" shouted CBS play-by-play man Brent Musburger. "Lakers win! Score it! Kareem Abdul-Jabbar has given the Lakers the victory and Magic Johnson is out there celebrating like they just won an NCAA championship!"**

And he was. He raced over to Kareem, jumped in his arms and hugged him tightly, exactly as he had hugged his college teammates.

**"All of us just kind of looked at him, like 'Yo, man, chill. We got 81 more games to go,'" remembered Norm Nixon.**

Magic never chilled; in fact, the opposite occurred. The cool Kareem warmed to Johnson's giddy college enthusiasm and with quality help from teammates Jamaal Wilkes and Nixon, the Lakers won the 1980 NBA title over Philadelphia. After the final game, Johnson celebrated again, acting almost as if the final game of the season was as important as the first.

## "TWO SECONDS, ONE SECOND ... WEST THROWS IT UP ... ,"

# WEST'S WING AND A PRAYER

*Should every great athletic moment be framed in victory for its true validation,*
*or does the sheer weight of the moment carry enough clout to define itself? Ponder that while*
*considering the majestic 60-foot shot that Jerry West swished through the net to send Game 3*
*of the 1970 NBA Finals into overtime against the New York Knicks. How does it stack up to*
*all other wondrous, heart-stopping moments?*

"... He makes it! West threw it up and makes it!"

"The man's crazy. He looks determined.
He thinks it's really going to go in."
CLYDE FRAZIER

Was the moment diminished because even after West scored 34 points in regulation, he then missed all five shots in overtime and his Los Angeles Lakers lost to the New York Knicks, 111-108? Does it matter that West's NBA Finals frustration would continue, losing his seventh straight trip to the championship? Or did his incredible moment stand alone, frozen forever in posterity?

**"West throws it up! He makes it! West threw it up and makes it!" New York Knicks announcer Bob Wolff shouted.**

After Knicks forward Dave DeBusschere made a driving jumper near the free throw line to put the Knicks ahead 102-100 with three seconds left in regulation, West took the inbounds pass under the basket, and immediately raced up court.

New York's 6-foot-10 center Willis Reed quickly rode up on West's left hip — all the while the voice of Wolff was capturing the moment for his listening and viewing audience.

"Two seconds, one second ... ," Wolff said, his voice even and emotionless.

Then Wolff's voice rose a bit as West became airborne from beyond the half-court circle, and launched a right-handed, high-high arching heave that seemed to disappear for a moment in the Forum rafters.

" ... *West throws it up ...* "

Then Wolff's voice went silent for what seemed like an eternity. Knicks guard Walt Frazier was standing near half-court and noticed something rather odd in West's expression as the ball began its descent.

"The man's crazy," Frazier remembered saying to himself. "He looks determined. He thinks it's really going to go in."

*"He makes it! West threw it up and makes it!"*

In that one instant, the Forum court was filled with bedlam for the home team and despair for the visitors. The Lakers ran to their bench in ecstasy; the Knicks were stunned. But only for a moment.

Ultimately, West's dramatic shot made no difference in the outcome of the game. But it did provide a jolt so profound that it still ranks as one of the most exciting moments in NBA history.

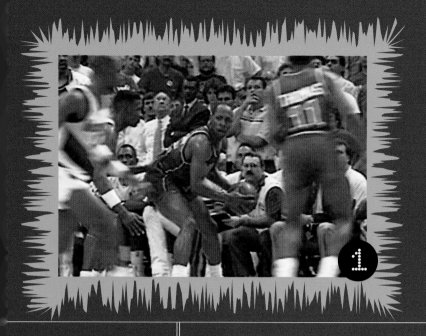

1990 NBA Finals, Game 5
DETROIT PISTONS 92,
PORTLAND
TRAIL BLAZERS 90
*JUNE 14, 1990*

# INSTANT VICTORY

## VINNIE JOHNSON, THE MICROWAVE, SHOOTS PISTONS TO TITLE

As Vinnie Johnson left the ground with the championship fate of the Detroit Pistons resting in his hands, his body was one big, twisted mess. If this was basketball as art, then Johnson was definitely an abstract Picasso.

His head, shoulders, hips, legs, elbows and wrists were all road signs at a seven-cornered crossroad, pointing in a half-dozen different directions. Johnson — whose offense was so scorching that he was christened "The Microwave" — was airborne and ready to unleash a last-second jump shot, even if he didn't look the part. "If anybody else had taken a shot so off-balanced, I might have been worried," said teammate Bill Laimbeer. "But not Vinnie. I've seen him make that kind of shot a thousand times. He's a playground player, a Brooklyn player, and that's the kind of shot he's always been able to make at any level he's played."

The result was one of the most dramatic shots in NBA history. When the ball passed through the hoop with seven-tenths of one second left, the Pistons had their second consecutive championship, becoming only the third franchise in NBA history to win back-to-back titles. For awhile, however, it looked like it would take longer.

With slightly less than three minutes remaining, the Trail Blazers held a 90-83 lead, but the Pistons went on a desperate rampage to tie the game at 90. With 20.1 seconds left, Detroit's future Hall of Fame point guard Isiah Thomas stood by the three-point line, carefully yo-yoing the ball. With Terry Porter defending tight to his hip, Thomas waited, probed, dribbled and looked at the clock. Seven seconds …

six seconds. He cut to the basket.

What would he do? Pass or shoot?

Thomas saw Johnson out of the corner of his eye. The closest defender to the 6-foot-2, quicksilver guard was 6-foot-7 forward Jerome Kersey. Isiah had his answer. Mismatch. Pass the ball to the Microwave. Vinnie took the pass with five seconds left, waited for a second, then drove hard to his left as Kersey back-peddled to defend a drive into the paint. But from 14 feet away, Johnson suddenly picked up the dribble, rose and fired up that odd-looking jumper.

Nothing but net.

"I dream about this all the time," Johnson said. "But I'm not usually in the game [at the end] so I don't get the opportunity. I guess you could say it's a dream come true."

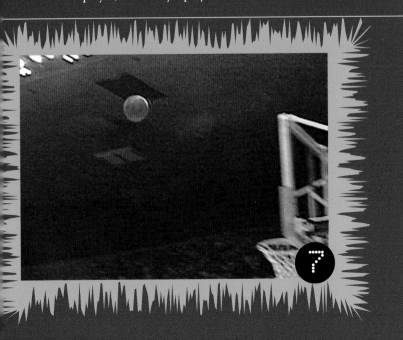

Avery Johnson had spent his entire basketball life dealing with doubters. **Some folks said he was too short, others said he couldn't shoot.** Plenty said he simply wasn't good enough to lead the San Antonio Spurs across the street, much less to an NBA title.

But the diminutive NBA vagabond answered all his critics in the 1999 NBA Finals against the New York Knicks. Johnson silenced 19,763 Madison Square Garden faithful by calmly sinking a game-winning 18-footer from the left corner with 47 seconds remaining in a 78-77 series-ending Game 5 victory that made the Spurs the first former ABA team to win an NBA crown since four ABA teams joined the NBA in 1976.

AVERY JOHNSON

CD1 TRACK 5

# THE SURVIVOR
## WINS THE BIG ONE

1999 NBA Finals, Game 5

[ SAN ANTONIO SPURS 78, NEW YORK KNICKS 77 ]

*JUNE 25, 1999*

"My whole life, not just on a basketball court but off the court is a big example to a lot of people out there," said Johnson. "They need to persevere in their own situations."

For the first six years of his pro basketball career, the 5-foot-11 guard bounced around five different NBA teams. He was cut twice by the Spurs — including once on the same day he'd been a groomsman in teammate David Robinson's wedding. Denver cut him on Christmas Eve. But the squeaky voiced point guard nicknamed the "Ghetto Preacher" kept coming back.

"It's been an example of just not really giving up, man, just hanging in there even when you get cut on Christmas Eve, just when the Spurs cut you on David Robinson's wedding day, after you were in the wedding," Johnson said moments

after he'd made the biggest shot of his life. "It's just unbelievable. I don't know what to say."

Johnson had defied the world, calmly stroking in a high-arching left-handed jumper for the game winner.

"In years past [his teammates] would pump fake the ball to me and shoot it," said Johnson. "But this year when I was open, they got me the ball. That really made me feel good."

It also made him a champion.

02:9

**MR. SMITH**
**GOES TO THE RECORD BOOK**

# The playground fantasy never changes.

*The ball is almost weightless, all but dancing on the ends of your fingertips. The release is smooth, the arc pure, the rotation of the ball's panels a rhapsody in slow motion. String music. Basketball's sweetest sound.*

## You do not miss. You cannot miss.

*With its last breath, the shot clock clicks to zero. The buzzer sounds. The crowd erupts.*

## You are the hero.

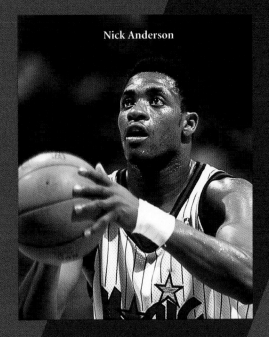

Nick Anderson

On the blacktops of Queens, underneath the netless rims always in need of fresh orange paint, Kenny Smith knew the melody by heart. But on the evening of June 7, 1995, fate challenged the Houston Rockets guard to the ultimate game of Name That Tune as Game 1 of the NBA Finals against the Orlando Magic dwindled to single digits.

**The dying clock showed 1.6 seconds left and the Rockets looking up at a three-point deficit as Smith took an inbounds pass, dribbled, pump-faked Orlando's Anfernee Hardaway, cradled the ball and prepared it for takeoff.** And an old, familiar refrain could be heard as the sphere cleanly snapped the net and sent the game to overtime.

While Smith gave the Rockets a chance to win, other vignettes also demanded the spotlight — Nick Anderson stunningly and inexplicably missing four consecutive free throws before Smith played hero; Hakeem Olajuwon tipping in a Clyde Drexler miss with three-tenths of a second remaining in overtime to give the Rockets a stirring 120-118 triumph.

The Magic never recovered. Houston went on to win the next three games and the sweep gave the Rockets their second consecutive title in four years.

"I'm excited about it," Smith said after his 23-point performance. "But I'm also realistic enough to realize what it really means. No one's going to remember 10 years from now how Kenny Smith played in Game 1. They're going to remember that Kenny Smith won and he was on the team that won. That's all they'll remember."

**Smith's humility was pleasant, but his prognostication was incorrect. That night, Smith made seven three-point baskets. No one has ever made more in an NBA Finals game. Of such performances, memories are made.**

---

**"No one's going to remember 10 years from now how Kenny Smith played in Game 1. They're going to remember that Kenny Smith won and he was on the team that won."**

**KENNY SMITH,** ON HIS 23-POINT PERFORMANCE

Memorial Auditorium, Dallas
[ INDIANA PACERS 119, DALLAS CHAPARRALS 118 ]
*NOVEMBER 13, 1967*

# AN ABA LONG-RANGE TREAT

## JERRY HARKNESS HITS A

# ·92-FOOTER·

### BY JAN HUBBARD

By the time he joined the Indiana Pacers in 1967, Jerry Harkness knew he was neither headed for the Hall of Fame, nor likely to receive major military honors. Yet one November night, Harkness created a moment for the ages, one of those rare records that may never be broken. It was a feat witnessed by few but destined for immortality.

With time running out in a game against the Dallas Chaparrals at Memorial Auditorium in Dallas, Harkness took an inbounds pass underneath the Pacers' defensive basket, turned, and launched the ball toward the heavens. The Chaps had taken a two-point lead on the previous play, and all that separated them from victory was an unanswered prayer.

It was the first year of the American Basketball Association and the season was only a month old. Determining that the NBA was classical music, the ABA went psychedelic, implementing such rock 'n' roll innovations as the red, white and blue basketball and the three-point shot. Each would impact the attempt by Harkness.

As the multi-colored ball soared through the air towards the opposite end, some in the crowd were mesmerized by the distinctiveness of the rapidly rotating colors. It was a slow-motion moment where three seconds seemed like 30.

**JERRY HARKNESS**

Ultimately, the ball went where no other had gone before, nor has gone since. It banked against the backboard, rattled both sides of the basket, and stunningly dropped through the net.

The basketball court is 94 feet long. *Harkness had made a 92-foot shot.*

At first, there was a dispute about whether time had expired, but ultimately, the referees said the shot counted. Everyone shrugged and prepared for overtime. But then the PA announcer said: "The basket is good. Because it was from behind the three-point line, it counts as three points. Pacers win, 119-118."

The crowd was shocked. Fans were not yet used to the three-point line, and the

shot had come from so far beyond it that no one connected the two.

Harkness was suddenly a legend in an unlikely role for a guy who would play in only 86 professional games.

"When I got home," said Harkness, who still lives in the Indianapolis area, "I was decorated by the Marines for rifle shooting [because of the shot]. That basketball has been in the Hall of Fame with my picture, but I have it now. That was my claim to fame, but it was really a lucky shot."

A blue spot was painted on the court where Harkness launched the shot, but when the Pacers came to Dallas on the next trip, Harkness noticed that the painted spot had been moved forward, and the record book says the shot was from 88 feet. "I remember being right under the basket," Harkness said.

One fan who agreed with him was a 19-year-old native of Dallas who was sitting in the upper deck that night behind Harkness and the basket. Years later, after a long career as a basketball journalist, that kid in the stands would join the NBA as the editor of publications, including this book.

Harkness was correct. I know, because I watched the basketball all the way. The shot was from 92 feet. And I've never taken a desperation shot for granted since.

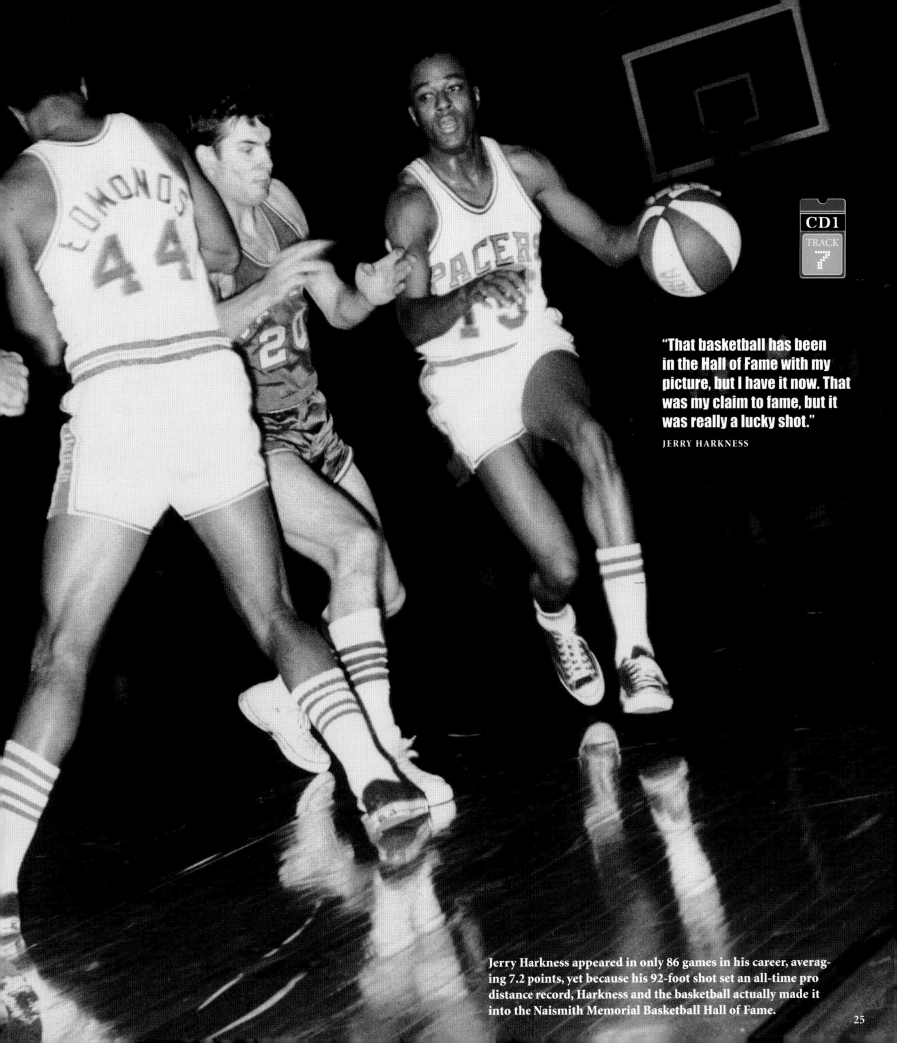

CD1
TRACK
7

"That basketball has been in the Hall of Fame with my picture, but I have it now. That was my claim to fame, but it was really a lucky shot."

JERRY HARKNESS

Jerry Harkness appeared in only 86 games in his career, averaging 7.2 points, yet because his 92-foot shot set an all-time pro distance record, Harkness and the basketball actually made it into the Naismith Memorial Basketball Hall of Fame.

25

"I've got one more three in me," said Elliott. And then he went out and proved it.

1999 Western Conference Finals, Game 2
[ SAN ANTONIO SPURS 86, PORTLAND TRAIL BLAZERS 85 ]
*May 31, 1999*

# SEAN ELLIOTT: SAN ANTONIO'S
# MIRACLE MAN

**From every corner of San Antonio's massive Alamodome, 35,260 spectators were taking a collective deep breath. Sean Elliott's feet hung precariously over the very edge of the sideline in the closing moments of Game 2 of the 1999 Western Conference Finals. He was performing the most delicate balancing act in the sports history of the hoop-crazy town.**

With little more than 10 seconds remaining, and the Spurs trailing the Portland Trail Blazers 85-83, Elliott took an inbounds pass from teammate Mario Elie that forced him within inches of the right sideline. In a split second, he had to regain his balance, his composure and his bearings as he navigated the sideline like a nervous tightrope walker in a turbulent storm. And, oh yes, he had to make the shot.

At that moment, Elliott was focused only on the task at hand, yet he had a troubling secret that he would not share with the public for almost two months, or until after the Spurs won the NBA championship. For seven years, Elliott had suffered from focal glomerulosclerosis, a kidney disorder. Elliott later admitted that he was persistently tired, but he had grown accustomed to dealing with the exhaustion.

With the game on the line, however, he had enough strength to not only catch the ball on his tiptoes, but also to go gracefully up into the air and release a three-point attempt over 6-foot-11 Rasheed Wallace, who was lunging to block the shot. The ball hit the bottom of the net with 9.9 seconds left, and the Spurs had stunned the Blazers. They went on to win the series in four consecutive games to advance to the Finals, where the Spurs defeated the New York Knicks in five games.

"If his heels had gone down, it would not have counted," said Spurs coach Gregg Popovich. "He must have had a feeling."

He must have had the feeling all game, because Elliott, who finished with 22 points, had already made five of six three-pointers before the game-winner.

He was the only outside scoring threat to help big men Tim Duncan (23 points, 10 rebounds, 5 blocked shots) and David Robinson (14 points, 7 boards, 3 steals, 3 blocked shots). The rest of the Spurs missed 29 of 39 shots from the floor.

During a timeout in the huddle before the final shot, Elliott was confident of success, telling his teammates, "I've got one more three in me." And then he went out and proved it.

As impressive as the shot was, the fact that Elliott was able to perform at such a high level while slowed by the kidney condition was even more amazing. In San Antonio, they referred to the shot as the "Memorial Day Miracle," but it was nothing compared to what would happen later. Elliott's brother Noel donated a kidney to Sean, who received the transplant on August 16, 1999. On

March 14, 2000, seven months later, after a determined rehabilitation program, Elliott returned to play, the only player in NBA history to come back after an organ transplant.

Sports are often overstated, equated to life and death, heroes and villains, war and peace. The Memorial Day Miracle has a nice ring to it and joyously captures a great shot and a great moment. But for Sean Elliott, the real miracle-worker in the Elliott family was brother Noel, who gave Sean the greatest assist of his life.

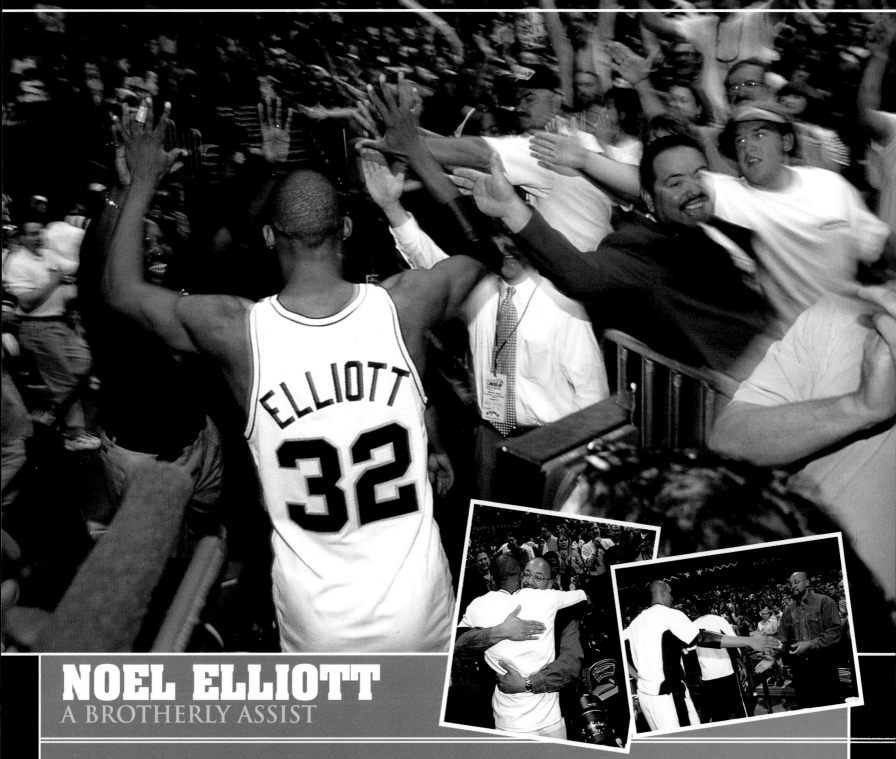

# NOEL ELLIOTT
## A BROTHERLY ASSIST

It clearly is the most unselfish move in the history of the NBA.

San Antonio's Sean Elliott had suffered from the kidney disorder focal glomerulosclerosis for seven years when he announced on July 21, 1999, that he needed a kidney transplant. So Elliott's brother Noel did what any sibling — he is one year older than Sean — would once blood tests showed he was a match: He donated one of his kidneys to Sean.

"I am both honored and glad that I can be here for my brother in his time of need," Noel said. "My brother has always been there for me, and I will always be there for him."

On August 16, 1999, doctors performed the transplant. Without a viable donor, Sean would have had to begin kidney dialysis in a matter of weeks. Three days later, Noel and Sean, side by side, appeared in public for the first time since the surgery.

"I've just got to be the best brother I can and take care of what he's given me," Sean said. "I'm just so proud. To be able to give a part of your body like that is an amazing sacrifice."

It also was the ultimate assist, although Noel did hint that, because some of the tests were so uncomfortable, there was a way for Sean to pay him back.

"I told Sean that I was going to have to have tickets to all the Spurs' games," Noel said. "*And* a book deal."

1993 Eastern Conference First Round, Game 4

**[ CHARLOTTE HORNETS 104, BOSTON CELTICS 103 ]**

*MAY 5, 1993*

# MOURNING'S MOMENT;

*One of the more vexing corollaries in all of professional sports is this somewhat callous fact of athletic life: The promising beginning of a young man's career often marks the bitter end for some noble, aging warrior. In the spring of 1993, that is how the lives and careers of rising Charlotte Hornets star Alonzo Mourning and the Celtics' champion graybeard Kevin McHale would intersect.*

## Time runs out on the Celtics

### McHale makes it official – and heroic

**On basketball**

**JACKIE MacMULLAN**

CHARLOTTE, N.C. - HE WANTed to do it on the court. Kevin McHale had this retirement thing all planned out: have a chat with the reporters who had covered him for years, tell a few jokes, remi— ...ll off the No. 32 jersey

at all. Thinking about retiring is one thing; saying it out loud is quite another.

Kevin McHale finally admitted it after the Celtics were eliminated by the Charlotte Hornets last night: His career is over. No more twisting scoops under the basket, no more arching fallaways, no more octopus rebounds, no more blocked shots, no more wisecracks.

No more pain.

"This has been a very tough year for me," he said. "I've had a lot of injuries, but this is the first time in my career I lost my mental edge. That was the really frustrating part.

cause I was afraid to get hurt. I was afraid of doing anything. I had to dig deep, deep, deep for what I gave in the playoffs."

He confirmed what we have suspected all along, that he made his decision to retire at the start of training camp. In fact, when McHale reported for the grueling preseason workouts, and his feet became wracked with pain within in days, he decided he would not play the 1992-93 season.

"It was hard, because my feet were really

**MORE ON NBA PLAYOFFS**

**EASTERN CONFERENCE**
Cleveland 93 ........ New Jersey 84
(Cavaliers lead series, 2-1)

**WESTERN CONFERENCE**
San Antonio 107 ..... Portland 101
(Spurs lead series, 2-1)
LA Clippers 93 ............ Houston 90
(Series tied, 2-2)

**Roundup, Page 54**

■ **Parish at end, too?** Chief suggests he may not be welcome back next year. Page 51.

■ **Alley-oops finish:** Brown hempans

### Mourning shot saves Charlotte

By Steve Fainaru
GLOBE STAFF

| Hornets 104 | CHARLOTTE, |
| Celtics 103 | N.C. - Celtic |

**G**ame 4 of the 1993 Eastern Conference first-round duel between the Hornets and Celtics would mark the start of a long, and mostly successful postseason road for Mourning. When the game ended, the 6-foot-10 rookie from Georgetown, was on the floor, flat on his back with his deliriously happy teammates piling on him. Mourning had made a 20-foot jumper with 0.4 seconds left for the 104-103 victory and a 3-1 series triumph.

As the 23-year-old Mourning celebrated, the 35-year-old McHale sat courtside, telling reporters that his Hall of Fame career had come to an end. "It's tough," McHale said, trying unsuccessfully to fight

back the tears. "All good things must come to an end. I really wanted to play one more game at the Boston Garden, but it wasn't meant to be. I wanted to go out like a warrior."

The 6-foot-10 power forward almost recaptured that old magic by helping Boston make up a 19-point deficit to take a one-point lead with less than 30 seconds remaining. Ultimately, however, it was Mourning's moment. And after helping the Celtics win three titles in the '80s, it was time for McHale to leave. He was troubled, no doubt, by the unfamiliar first-round loss, but, despite his view to the contrary, he was also every bit the warrior he longed to be, and always had been.

> **"ALL GOOD THINGS MUST COME TO AN END. I REALLY WANTED TO PLAY ONE MORE GAME AT THE BOSTON GARDEN, BUT IT WASN'T MEANT TO BE. I WANTED TO GO OUT LIKE A WARRIOR."**
>
> **KEVIN McHALE**

# McHALE'S LAMENT

1997 Western Conference Finals, Game 6

**[ UTAH JAZZ 103, HOUSTON ROCKETS 100 ]**

*MAY 29, 1997*

**MORE SPORTS**

■ Hingis survives scare: Page 3B

■ Dale Robertson: Page 3B

■ Graham's methods work: Page 3B

**ROCKETS**

*EXTRA*

**ROCKETS**

ROCKETS VS. JAZZ: GAME 8

**BEREAVE IT**

FRIDAY, MAY 30, 1997

Buzzer-beating 3 by Stockton puts end to Rockets

1997 NBA PLAYOFFS

CHRONICLE / SECTION B ★★

# Rocket

# Launcher

## Stockton's Shot Sends Jazz to Finals

*In the long playoff history of the Utah Jazz, the most familiar sound heard was the frustrating groan of another postseason ending without fulfillment. As the game-ending buzzer wailed in The Summit in Houston following Game 6 of the 1997 Western Conference Finals, however, at long last the Jazz finally heard basketball's sweetest sounds.*

> "These guys have been criticized the last few years for not getting to where we're going, but I've always said the most important thing in sports is to keep trying. Let this be an example of what it means to say it's never over." **JERRY SLOAN**, Utah Jazz head coach

**I**t was the string music of John Stockton swishing in a 25-foot jumper that gave the Jazz a 103-100 victory over the Houston Rockets and sent the Jazz into the NBA Finals for the first time in franchise history.

Since Stockton and Malone joined the Jazz in 1984 and 1985, respectively, **the team had steadily improved to become one of the best in the Western Conference. Between 1988-89 and**

**1996-97, in fact, no team in the West won more games than the Jazz.** Yet despite eight seasons of 50 or more victories, Utah was never able to get past the conference finals. So while Portland, Houston, Seattle, Los Angeles and Phoenix had all reached the NBA Finals during that period, the Jazz was building a reputation as disappointing playoff underachievers.

That disappeared with a bit of last-minute heroics by Stockton, who scored

13 of his team-high 25 points in the final 3:13, including that one stunning bit of game-winning string music. Until the very end, it did not look promising for Utah, and Houston seemed close to forcing a seventh game. With about seven minutes left, Houston had a 13-point lead.

The Jazz proved to be resilient, however, and even though Utah could not defeat the Chicago Bulls in the NBA Finals, the team at least made it to the big dance.

# THE LIBERTY HAS LANDED

**CD1**
TRACK
**11**

**1999 WNBA Championship, Game 2**
**NEW YORK LIBERTY 68,**
**HOUSTON COMETS 67**
*SEPTEMBER 4, 1999*

## T-Spoon's Dramatic 50-footer

In the brief history of the Women's National Basketball Association, two distinctive exploits are representative of championship life in the WNBA: the Houston Comets' domination, and Teresa Weatherspoon's miraculous buzzer beater from beyond the midcourt line.

On the way to their third consecutive WNBA crown, the Comets seemed poised for a celebration in the closing seconds of Game 2 of the 1999 WNBA Championship. They had already won Game 1 of the best-of-three series against the New York Liberty, and with 2.4 seconds left, Houston's Tina Thompson took a pass from Cynthia Cooper and converted a spinning bank shot to give the Comets a 67-65 lead. That sent the 16,285 home-town fans inside the Compaq Center into a frenzy.

All along the Comets' bench, Houston players were dancing and jumping and high-fiving each other, believing that in a few seconds they would be crowned with their third consecutive WNBA title.

But Teresa Weatherspoon had another plan. Standing in front of the Comets' bench, she caught Kym Hampton's inbounds pass, then with Thompson clinging to her left hip, T-Spoon took two dribbles, took off about five feet behind half-court and heaved a right-handed prayer at the basket from more than 50 feet away.

As the ball rose in the air, the spectators seemed to be preparing themselves for one

"When it left my hand it just looked like it was going in."

TERESA WEATHERSPOON

# GIVE THEM LIBERTY

## Teresa keeps hope alive with half-court miracle

of those deep, passionate explosions in anticipation of a championship celebration. The ushers and security officers were already lining the court with rope to keep the fans from mobbing the Comets on the floor. But the ball descended on a straight line, smacked against the backboard, and ricocheted perfectly through the net.

The Houston explosion turned into numbed, disbelieving silence. The Liberty had won Game 2, tying the best-of-three series.

"When it left my hand it just looked like it was going in," said Weatherspoon, who flopped on the floor and jackknifed her arms and legs out to fully embrace all her stunned and delirious teammates as they piled on top of her at half-court.

A few paces away, Tina Thompson stood there with her mouth wide open. Her eyes were as wide as two moons as she stared helplessly at the rim and then she said the one word that seemed to sum it all up for everyone who had just seen T-Spoon's half-court miracle.

"What??!!"

It proved to be a temporary setback for the Comets, who would win Game 3 and their third title. The Shot, however, is something that not only the Liberty and Weatherspoon will never forget, but hoops aficionados also will always remember. Because, simply stated, it was one of the most dramatic shots in the history of professional basketball by anyone.

# Impossible!

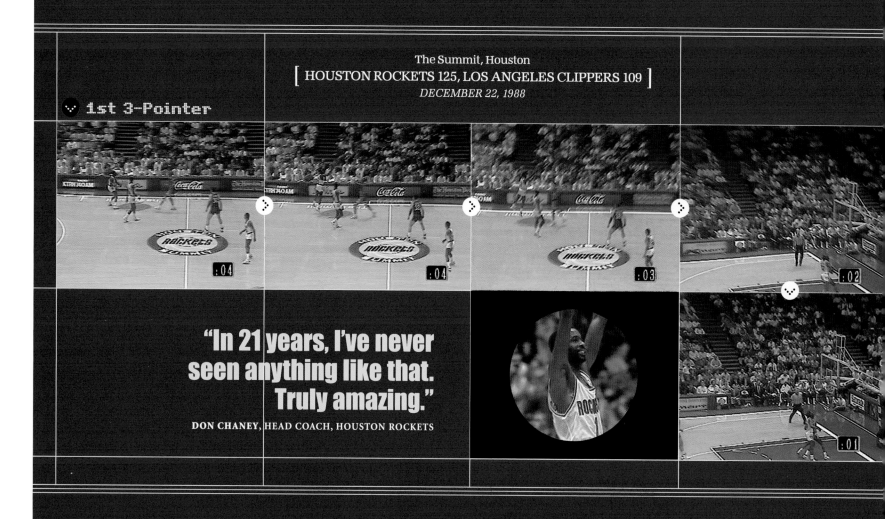

The Summit, Houston

[ HOUSTON ROCKETS 125, LOS ANGELES CLIPPERS 109 ]

*DECEMBER 22, 1988*

1st 3-Pointer

:04  :04  :03  :02

"In 21 years, I've never seen anything like that. Truly amazing."

**DON CHANEY,** HEAD COACH, HOUSTON ROCKETS

:01

In its most glorious form, basketball turns the ordinary into the extraordinary. In an instant, a reticent crowd becomes raucous because of a spectacular dunk. A standard fast break becomes a legendary film clip because a great point guard makes an astonishing pass. A highly skilled player makes a last second shot from half-court look almost as easy as a two-foot tap-in.

# TWO THREE-POINTERS IN ONE SECOND?

CD1
TRACK
12

2nd 3-Pointer

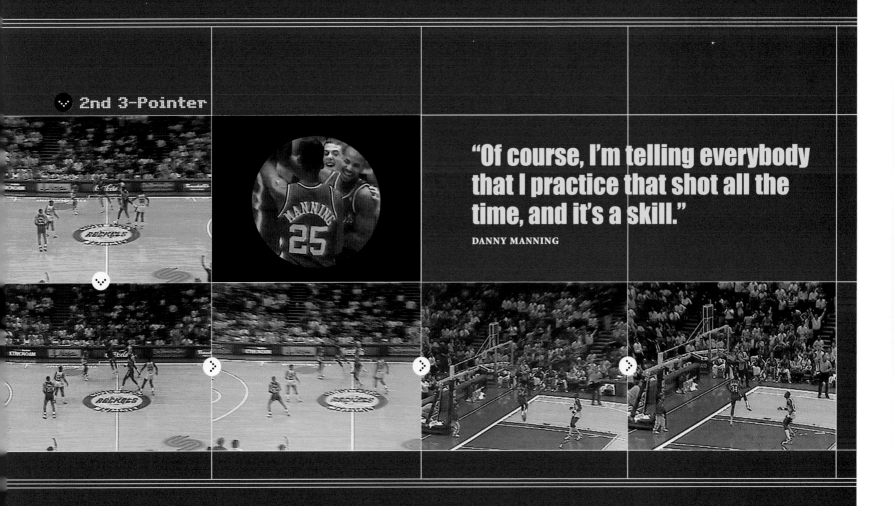

"Of course, I'm telling everybody that I practice that shot all the time, and it's a skill."
DANNY MANNING

On December 22, 1988, an early-season game between the Houston Rockets and Los Angeles Clippers turned into an unforgettable event. In the final seconds of the third quarter, Houston led 85-78 and Rockets forward Buck Johnson lofted a desperation shot from 55 feet. One second was left on the clock. The ball hit the backboard and went through the basket.

Rockets fans went wild while Clippers center Greg Kite retrieved the ball. The clock had stopped for the throw-in. Kite spotted rookie forward Danny Manning, who was near half-court. Before the buzzer sounded to end the period, Manning launched a shot from 43 feet away.

Nothing but net.

"That was in my younger days," Manning said recently. "It was a lot of fun to see two back-to-back shots go in. Of course, I'm telling everybody that I practice that shot all the time, and it's a skill. And they're like, 'Yeah, right.'"

Records of this sort are not kept, but it is probably safe to say that never in an NBA game have two shots near half court been made in less than a second.

"There have been a lot of spectacular plays in the NBA," Manning said. "It's fun to have been a part of one like that."

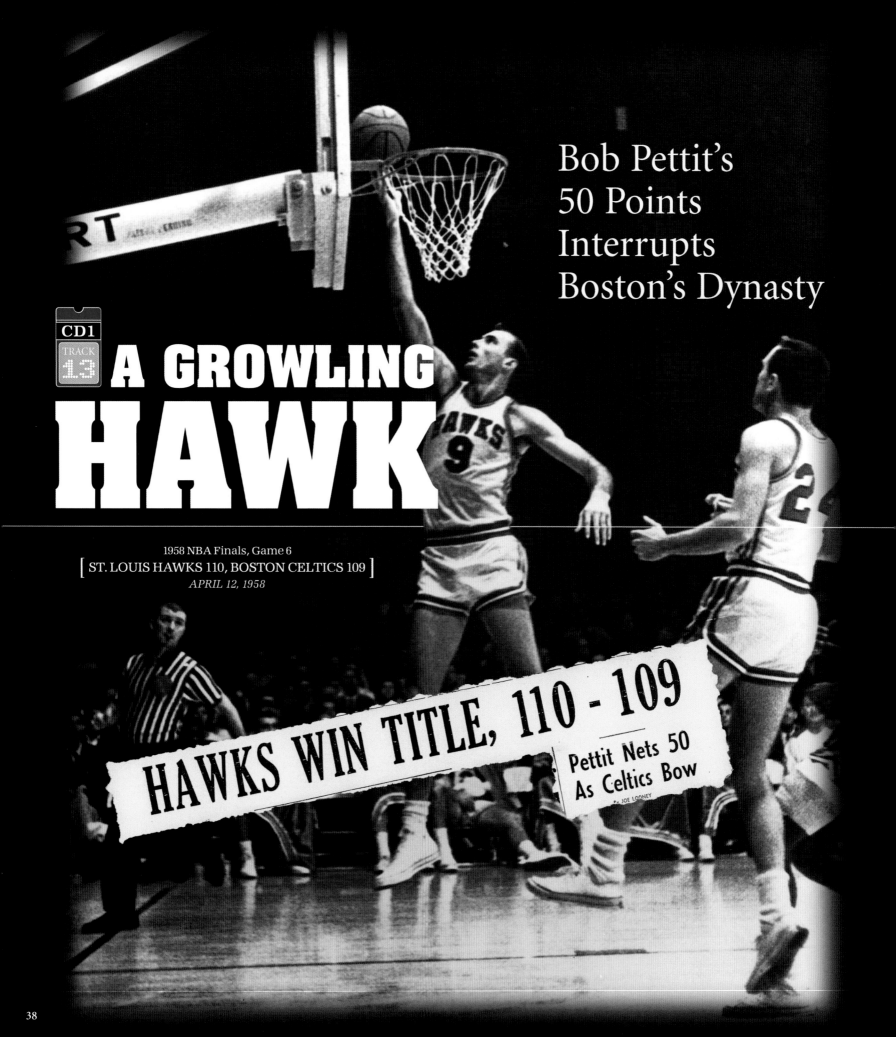

Bob Pettit's
50 Points
Interrupts
Boston's Dynasty

# A GROWLING HAWK

1958 NBA Finals, Game 6
[ ST. LOUIS HAWKS 110, BOSTON CELTICS 109 ]
*APRIL 12, 1958*

HAWKS WIN TITLE, 110 - 109

Pettit Nets 50
As Celtics Bow

BY JOE LOONEY

*Winning NBA titles during the late 1950s and early 1960s was about as easy as landing on the moon — except, of course, for the Boston Celtics. To this day, their record is staggering. Beginning in 1959, the Celtics won eight consecutive titles, nine in 10 years and 11 in 13 years.*

*The first of the two interruptions of their dynasty occurred only because of a record-setting performance by a man who learned early in life that overcoming the odds required, very simply, a mean streak. Or, as Bob Pettit of Baton Rouge, La., would say in the descriptive vernacular of his region:*

## "WHEN I FALL BELOW WHAT I KNOW I CAN DO, MY BELLY GROWLS AND GROWLS."

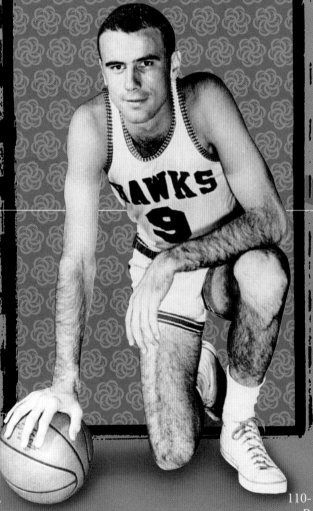

19 58

That visceral intensity, along with a rugged, angular body and a deadly shooting eye, made the 6-9, 215-pound Pettit one of the dominant players of the early NBA. In a career highlighted by 10 selections to the All-NBA First Team, Pettit had gaudy averages of 26.4 points and 16.2 rebounds. In 1970, he was enshrined in the Naismith Memorial Basketball Hall of Fame. In 1996, he was selected as one of the 50 Greatest Players in NBA History.

It took a man with these impeccable credentials and extraordinary talent to disrupt the Celtics' machine. The Celtics won their first championship in 1957, but it took them seven tough games to defeat Pettit's St. Louis Hawks. Game 7, in fact, went into double overtime and the Celtics won by two points.

So defeating the Celtics would require a monumental performance, and that's exactly what the Hawks got from Pettit in the 1958

NBA Finals. The Hawks led the series three games to two with Game 6 in St. Louis.

Pettit, as they say, came to play. After three quarters, he had 31 points, but the best was yet to come. In the last quarter, Pettit scored 19 of his team's final 21 points, including a tip-in with 15 seconds remaining that gave the Hawks a three-point cushion 110-107. They went on to survive 110-109, winning their only NBA title.

Pettit finished with 50 points, establishing a then-NBA Finals record for most points in a game.

**"He would play all out, whether he was 50 points ahead, or 50 points behind,"** Boston coach Red Auerbach said of Pettit. **"It didn't matter. That's the only way he knew how to play — all out."**

To beat the Celtics, he had to. Boston went on to win the next eight championships.

MOST POINTS IN AN NBA FINALS GAME
**50 POINTS**
BOB PETTIT
THEN - NBA FINALS RECORD

1998 NBA Finals, Game 6
[ CHICAGO BULLS 87, UTAH JAZZ 86 ]
*JUNE 14, 1998*

# CHAPTER 2
# MICHAEL & THE JORDANAIRES: MORE GREAT SHOTS

## A DYNASTY OF GREAT MOMENTS

Michael Jordan was an astonishing force of nature, a man who had turned his hoop life
into arguably the greatest athletic drama in pro basketball history. MJ — and often,
his supporting cast, the Jordanaires, if you will — surely
knew how to provide compelling touches to so many championship moments.

So it only seemed fitting that the denouement of Jordan's career as a Bull would
be this consummate moment — championship on the line, final seconds ticking down in Game 6
of the 1998 NBA Finals, the whole world knowing he would shoot.

## His final shot is so poignant.

Jordan suspended in midair, seemingly posing for posterity for that sea of
petrified Utah Jazz fans, and that lone, prescient Bulls fan who was waiting for the
inevitable string music.

For MJ, the ultimate drama king, striking that pose was his way of reminding us that the
Jordan Chronicles were unparalleled.

## Michael Jordan always was the last man standing.

### OTHER CHAPTER 2 MOMENTS

Jordan Soars ... Scores ... And Roars!

Moment of Glory
Steve Kerr Wins a Championship

Paxson Beats Suns

MJ's Revenge
Torches Celtics for 63

Six Times as Sweet
MJ Rains Threes on Portland

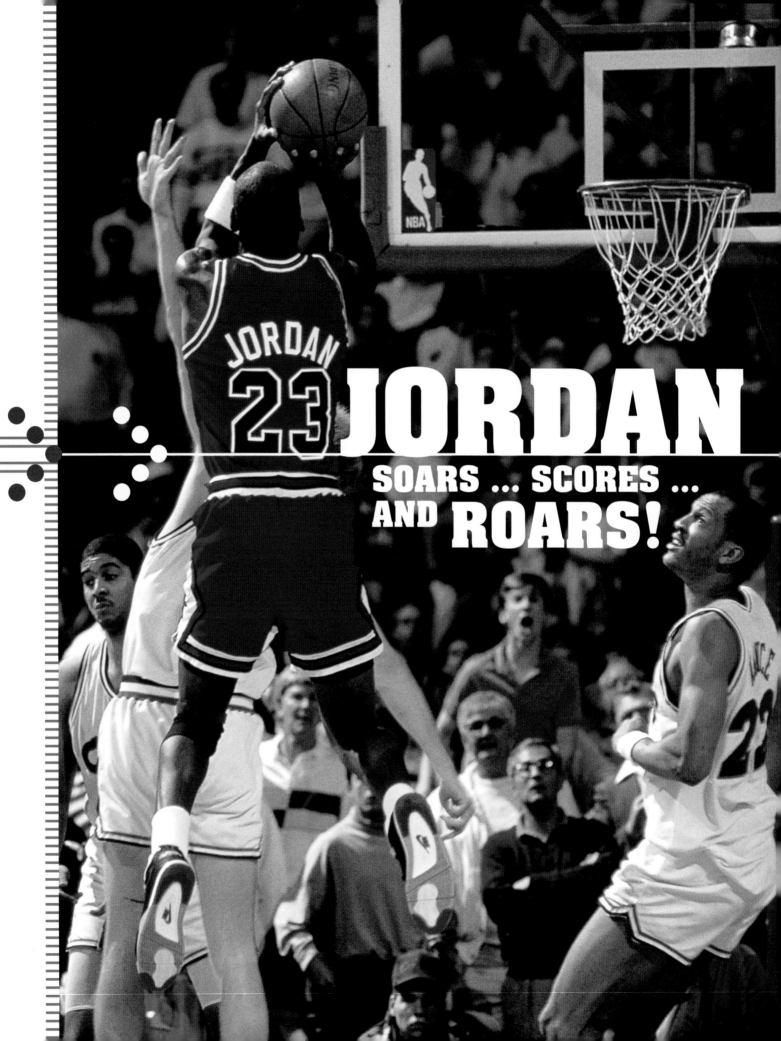

[
*In the formative days of his wondrous legend, Michael Jordan was viewed as nothing more substantial than a dreamy vision of athletic pleasure. The young Air Jordan was part gravity-defying stylist, part New Age pitchman; a cartoon superhero capable of swooping down from the heavens with a round ball in one hand and a soft drink in the other.*
]

But all of that changed on May 7, 1989, when the basketball world was first fully exposed to the other side of His Airness' growing legend — the cold-blooded, win-at-all-costs competitor. That was the moment when a raging Jordan stood in the middle of Richfield Coliseum pumping his fists and lacing the air with angry expletives after sinking a hanging jumper at the buzzer to help the Chicago Bulls defeat the Cleveland Cavaliers 101-100. It was the fifth and deciding game of the NBA Eastern Conference First Round, and the Bulls stunned the heavily favored Cavaliers to advance to the next round.

The moment endures to this day. With three seconds left, Jordan got the ball, craftily pushed away 6-foot-10 defender Larry Nance, took three dribbles to his left and arrived at the top of the key, where he met Cleveland's Craig Ehlo. While Jordan made the game-winning shot 25 times during his NBA career (24 in the last 10 seconds of games), none demonstrated his superior athleticism more than this jump shot that advanced the notion of hang time to implausible levels. Jordan and Ehlo went up at the same time, but long after Ehlo had descended, Jordan was still suspended in midair, waiting to be completely clear, and finally releasing a picture-perfect shot.

The shot was nothing but sweet, and afterward, Jordan was the opposite. As the ball swished through the basket, he pumped his fists in mad celebration, shouting at the top of his lungs an expletive-laced rant. "Go Home, #@%! Go Home!," he screamed.

"I can't believe he hit that shot," said Cleveland center Brad Daugherty, Jordan's former teammate at the University of North Carolina. "I don't know how he stayed in the air that long."

As the Cavaliers and the rest of the NBA were about to discover, Jordan — when properly motivated — could do quite a few unbelievable things.

"That's probably the biggest shot I've had in the NBA, mainly because I had put my credibility on the line," Jordan said at

> "That's probably the biggest shot I've had in the NBA, mainly because I had put my credibility on the line. I had said we could beat this team."
>
> MICHAEL JORDAN

the time. "I had said we could beat this team."

The Cavaliers, at 57-25, had tied for the second-best record in the league, and had beaten Jordan's Bulls in all six regular-season meetings. But Jordan prophesied that his Bulls, who finished fifth in the Central Division at 47-35, would beat the Cavaliers in four games in the best-of-five series. Chicago won Game 1 and Game 3, but in Game 4 at home, the Bulls lost in overtime 108-105. Jordan scored 50 points but missed two free throws in the final 48 seconds of regulation.

On the morning of Game 5, Jordan read the Cleveland sports section in his hotel room. One article caught his attention. Some Cavaliers players were quoted as saying they would "send the Bulls home" with

# the shot

a series-clinching victory. That was the first lesson the rest of the NBA learned. Don't provide Michael with any extra incentive. The guy is motivated to an almost frightening level. Why unnecessarily feed the monster?

Game 5 would remain close throughout, but with only three seconds left, the Cavaliers had taken a 100-99 lead. In the huddle, Bulls coach Doug Collins drew up a very simple play: "That play was 'Give the ball to Michael and everyone else get the #@@#%* out of the way,'" Collins joked afterward.

Just before the Bulls broke the huddle, Jordan looked at point guard Craig Hodges. "He just told me, 'Don't worry about it. I'm going to drop this one,'" Hodges said.

The way Jordan saw it, he had no choice but to make the shot, because he was still haunted by those missed free throws from Game 4. "I knew I was going to shoot a jump shot," said Jordan. "I wasn't too confident about my free throws. I said, 'I can't go to the line again, here.'"

Ready and confident, Jordan went out to shoot what became known as "The Shot." It would torment a generation of Cavaliers fans while giving everyone the first real glimpse of his ruthless competitive nature.

It would be two more seasons before Jordan's championship cravings would be satisfied. But as he stood there pumping his fists and ranting against the entire basketball world, it was our first warning that the 26-year-old Jordan was transforming himself into an insatiable competitive hunter.

1997 NBA Finals, Game 6
[ CHICAGO BULLS 90, UTAH JAZZ 86 ]
*JUNE 13, 1997*

# MOMENT *of*

*The scoreboard clock inside Chicago's United Center might as well have put it in lights.*
*The Bulls and Utah Jazz were tied at 86 with less than 20 seconds remaining in Game 6 of the NBA Finals,*
*and a championship was on the line. Everybody knew what was going to happen — the Bulls, the Jazz, the announcers,*
*the press, the fans and the guy who ran the scoreboard.*

## *"It's Michael Jordan time," said NBC's Marv Albert, and Jordan agreed,*
## *"Everybody in the gym, everybody on TV knew it was coming to me," he said.*

**I**n the huddle, Jordan glanced to his left at Steve Kerr, the man he knew would ultimately embody the critical moment. "I looked at Steve and said, '**This is your chance,**'" said Jordan. "'**I know Stockton is going to come over and help and I'm going to come to you.**'"

Kerr was a career journeyman unaccustomed to the role of last-second hero. He'd spent his entire career as a bit player, and in this championship series had missed several critical shots. But when Jordan told him to look for his shot, **Kerr looked confidently back at His Airness and said, "I'll be ready, I'll knock it down."**

The play went exactly as Michael envisioned. After running through a series of screens and cutting behind Scottie Pippen toward the top of the key, Jordan had the ball. With Bryon Russell defending and Stockton lingering to MJ's right, Jordan dribbled left, drawing the predicted double team.

"It is Michael Jordan time," Albert said. "Scottie Pippen looking for Michael Jordan … checks the clock … 5 on the 24 … here's Jordan."

Jordan split between Russell and Stockton, first faking a shot, then a pass in the far corner to Toni Kukoc, who was spotting up for a three-pointer. The fake drew in Utah guard Jeff Hornacek, who skipped toward Kukoc instead of rotating to the top to pick up Kerr, who was left wide open.

**Kerr calmly shot himself into NBA immortality by stroking in a swishing game-winner with five seconds left, and the enormity of the accomplishment was not lost upon him.**

"I'm just so thankful to be able to be a teammate of Michael's," said Kerr. "He's so good that he draws so much attention. His Excellency gave me the chance to hit the game-winning shot in the NBA Finals. What a thrill. And I owe him everything."

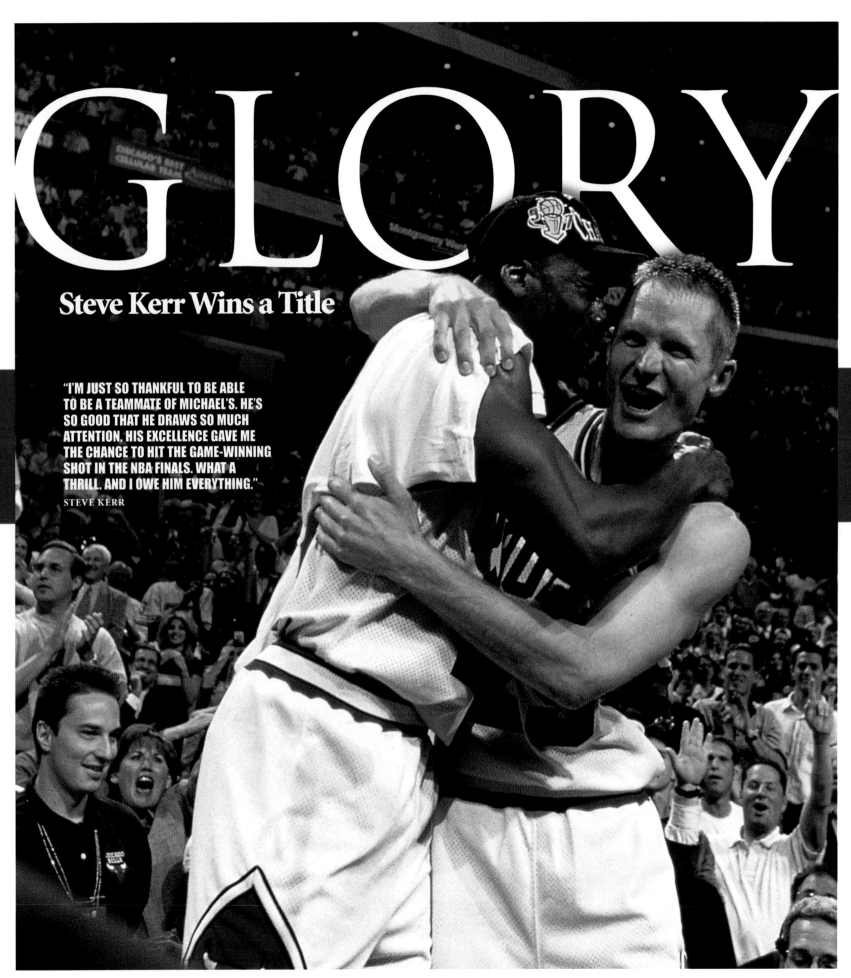

# GLORY

## Steve Kerr Wins a Title

"I'M JUST SO THANKFUL TO BE ABLE TO BE A TEAMMATE OF MICHAEL'S. HE'S SO GOOD THAT HE DRAWS SO MUCH ATTENTION. HIS EXCELLENCE GAVE ME THE CHANCE TO HIT THE GAME-WINNING SHOT IN THE NBA FINALS. WHAT A THRILL. AND I OWE HIM EVERYTHING."
STEVE KERR

# PAXSON BEATS SUNS

*There was a delightful simplicity to the moment for John Paxson. Spotting up for the biggest jump shot of his life in the crazed final seconds of Game 6 of the 1993 NBA Finals, he had no time to be overwhelmed by the circumstances of the moment. Paxson's only focus was on the pure mechanics of a jump shot. They never changed with the environment, no matter how big the game.*

## NO DEFENDER CLOSE. SET YOUR FEET. GO STRAIGHT UP. ELBOW IN. SEE THE RIM. SNAP YOUR WRIST.

Sw

## "It seemed like that ball was in the air for about an hour."

**PAUL WESTPHAL,** Phoenix Suns Head Coach

"**Y**ou catch it and shoot," said Paxson. **"It's a shot I've practiced hundreds of thousands of times in my driveway growing up."**

So it hardly mattered that with 5.3 seconds remaining and his Chicago Bulls trailing the Phoenix Suns, 98-96, the championship was in his hands. Phoenix defenders had denied Michael Jordan and Scottie Pippen with strong defense and swarming triple teams. So the ball went from MJ to Pippen and from Pippen to Horace Grant. But Grant — who had missed a layup moments earlier — decided that he wouldn't risk missing another one. So the 6-foot-10 forward passed up a shot under the hoop to kick it out to Paxson, who was outside the three-point line.

No defender close. Set your feet. Go straight up. Elbow in. See the rim. Snap your wrist.

As he released the ball, there seemed to be a vacuum in America West Arena, sucking up every sound and emotion, everyone breathlessly waiting for the ball to descend. "It seemed like that ball was in the air for about an hour," said Phoenix head coach Paul Westphal.

Finally, with 3.9 seconds left … swissshhh!

Bulls 99-98. Their first three-peat.

"Horace did the right thing," said Jordan. "His confidence was shot." Paxson's confidence was not. He knew the Suns would collapse on Chicago's Big Three, so he lurked beyond the three-point line, "just in case something happened." That "something" did happen, and Paxson was ready.

Set your feet. Go straight up. Elbow in. See the rim. Snap your wrist.

**"It's all instinct," Paxson said.**

# issShhh!

### JOHN PAXSON:
### MESSAGE TO ALICE COOPER —
# SCHOOL'S OUT

"In 1993, I had a chance to make one of the most memorable plays in the history of the NBA Finals. John Paxson was literally about two feet away from me when he took his three-point shot with a couple of seconds remaining in Game 6. When he got the ball, the thought went through my head, 'Do I trip him?' I decided not to because I thought he couldn't make it.

Of course, he did and the Bulls defeated my Phoenix Suns for the NBA title. And even though we lost, I made the right decision, because if I had tripped him, the NBA would have banned me from games for life.

But I would have been a hero in Phoenix. And what about that headline possibility? 'Alice Cooper to Bulls: No More Mr. Nice Guy.'"

**ALICE COOPER,**
**MR. NICE GUY AND PHOENIX SUNS SUPERFAN**

"I think he's God disguised as Michael Jordan."
LARRY BIRD

# M.J.'S REVENGE

## AINGE BEATS JORDAN AT GOLF; M.J. TORCHES CELTICS FOR 63

### BY DANNY AINGE

*In 1986, I was playing on a Boston Celtics team led by Larry Bird, Kevin McHale and Robert Parish, and I still believe it is one of the best in the history of the league. We felt like we were going to win the championship, and we did, but I suppose that confident feeling kind of allowed us to take other teams for granted, at least in the early rounds of the playoffs.*

We were playing the Bulls in the first round, so when Mike Carey, who covered the Celtics for the *Boston Herald*, asked me if I wanted to play golf on an off day with Michael Jordan and Mark Vancil, a reporter for the *Chicago Sun-Times*, I said sure.

Michael was just taking up golf and had been getting lessons from Davis Love III, so I knew he loved to play. But on that day, I had the better game and beat him, which, of course, he wasn't too happy about. Michael always was one of the great trash-talkers on the court, and he was the same way on the golf course. He just couldn't back it up quite as well.

Our defensive specialist at the time was Dennis Johnson, who was a great player. But when we dropped Michael off at the hotel, he was still ticked about losing in golf, and he told me:

## "Tell your man D.J. I got something for him tomorrow."

The next day, Michael scored 63, which is still the record for the playoffs. We won the game in double overtime, but watching him that day was incredible. D.J. picked up his fourth foul midway through the third quarter and I was in foul trouble the entire second half. Larry, Kevin and Robert all took swipes at him, Bill Walton played 25 minutes in that game and he fouled out — Michael just made our defense look helpless.

Larry said it best later: "I think he's God disguised as Michael Jordan."

Everyone knew Michael was an excellent player, but I think that was the first time everyone realized how great he was. I know I certainly learned a lesson:

I should not have beaten him in golf.

# MJ RAINS THREE

# SIX TIMES AS SWEET

Someone could read every tome penned on the workings of the mind and its effect on the body it commands, and there would not be an explanation for every phenomenon. There are words that seek to explain – such as destiny, fate, providence ... and even, luck.

Michael Jordan can't really say what it was, although in retrospect, there were several clues to be had on the afternoon of June 3, 1992. That night, the Chicago Bulls would play the Portland Trail Blazers in Game 1 of the NBA Finals. During the day, Jordan set a personal record when he bench-pressed 265 pounds. He was feeling strong.

Later, he spent an hour propelling three-pointers with Buzz Peterson, his college roommate. Jordan said it was a playful sort of practice, "Shooting with our eyes closed and left-handed and stuff." But he was making far more than he missed, so he was feeling precise.

Then there was the pregame interview with Marv Albert, who would call the game with Mike Fratello and Magic Johnson. "We had talked to him before the game about shooting threes," Albert said. "Michael's one of these guys who would say, 'Today I'm going to be an assist guy,' 'Today I'm going to do this,' – you know, control the game. And he said he felt he had to shoot

threes." He was feeling like a prophet.

And he was. Jordan shot threes so effortlessly, he probably co[uld] have shot them with his eyes closed. He had six three-pointers, s[et] an NBA Finals record by scoring 35 points in the first half, and w[as] so amazed by his proficiency that he looked almost apologetic. A[fter] his sixth three-pointer, Jordan locked eyes [with] the NBC broadcast crew.

"He gave that expression when he look[ed] over to the table," Albert said. "He shrugge[d,] like, 'I can't believe I'm doing this.'"

Little was needed from Jordan the rest [of] the game as the Bulls battered Portland, 12[2-] 89. Jordan ended the night with 39 and ev[en] though the Blazers put up a valiant fight, [the] Bulls went on to win the title in six games[. It] was their second of six championships in [the] 1990s.

Even Jordan marveled at his own perfo[rm-] ance. **"I've never had a game like that in t[he] Finals,"** he said. **"Given the importance o[f the] game, it was probably my best game ever. I don't know what I could do for an encore."**

He would eventually find out, but even four additional titles never blotted out the brilliance of the shooting exhibition that night in a rumbling old Chicago Stadium.

# ON PORTLAND

"I've never had a game like that in the Finals. Given the importance of the game, it was probably my best game ever. I don't know what I could do for an encore."

MICHAEL JORDAN

1994 NBA Finals, Game 6
[ HOUSTON ROCKETS 86, NEW YORK KNICKS 84 ]
*June 19, 1994*

"I can't believe he was going for a three-pointer. He has no conscience."

HAKEEM OLAJUWON

# CHAPTER 3

# GREAT MOVES

# CHAMPIONSHIP DENIAL

## HAKEEM BLOCKS N.Y.'S TITLE DREAMS

John Starks had been in one of those deliciously unconscious grooves that sweeps over a streak shooter's body. With 16 of his 27 points coming in the fourth quarter, Starks was brimming with confidence, certain that anything released from his fingertips would hit nothing but net.

Unfortunately for Starks, another man was in a groove of his own — Houston center Hakeem Olajuwon. Playing with five fouls for most of the fourth quarter of Game 6 of the 1994 NBA Finals, Olajuwon was on a defensive streak. When the 6-foot-5 Starks rose from the floor with six seconds left in the game, he had a chance to give New York the victory and the title. But Olajuwon did his imitation of a space shuttle blastoff, springing from the court and stretching his 7-foot body to the maximum.

# Blocked shot. Ball game.

Starks' attempt at a three-pointer for the game-winner fluttered harmlessly to the floor and the Rockets won 86-84. The Rockets thus tied the series, then went on to win Game 7 and the championship. Great moves are often offensive, but the Rockets had no doubt that the key move in securing their first of two titles was a defensive masterpiece.

## OTHER CHAPTER 3 MOMENTS

DR. J and the Ultimate Hangtime
Move

The 1991 Move
An MJ Spectacular

Sampson to the Rescue!
Buzzer Beater Boosts Rockets

Bird in Flight
Larry's Legendary Move

Horsing Around
Freddie Lewis Wins All-Star MVP

Train to Nowhere
On the Road in the Early NBA

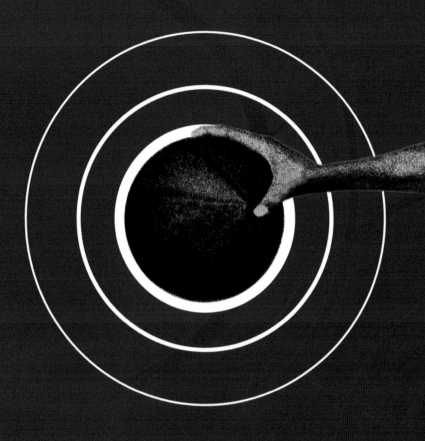

1980 NBA Finals, Game 4
[ PHILADELPHIA 76ERS 105, LOS ANGELES LAKERS 102 ]
*MAY 11, 1980*

# D.R. J

## and the Ultimate Hangtime Move

### THE NOTION OF DEFYING GRAVITY HAS EVOLVED FROM A SINGULARLY WONDROUS RARE EVENT TO A REGULAR OCCURRENCE THAT IS TAKEN FOR GRANTED.

CD 1

TRACK
21

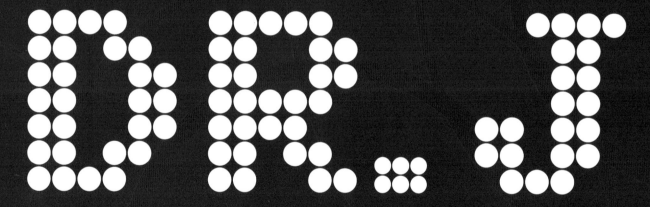

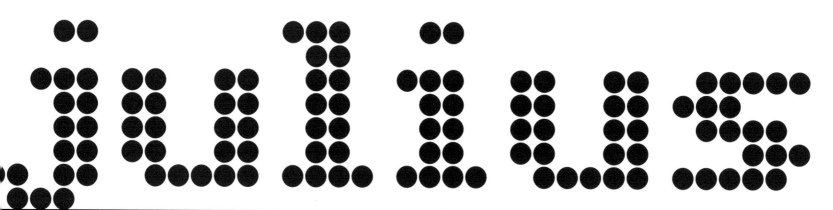

# JULIUS

**"... WE CUT HIM OFF AND THERE WAS NOWHERE FOR HIM TO GO BUT OUT OF BOUNDS ..."**

Today's NBA games often resemble the skies around a major airport with powerful athletes soaring, hovering, dunking and landing with breathtaking elegance. **Every phenomenon has its roots, and although players such as Elgin Baylor and Connie Hawkins first orbited the air above the rim, it was Julius Erving, the Doctor, who went to the moon.**

In Game 4 of the 1980 NBA Finals at the Spectrum in Philadelphia, Erving not only defied gravity, but also violated every reasonable sensibility of what a man is capable of doing in midair with a basketball in his hand. Dribbling toward the right baseline against the Los Angeles Lakers, Erving lifted off the ground, ready to attack. Always the space seeker, the Doctor spotted a crease of daylight on the other side of the basket as he became airborne. As Erving rose, Lakers defenders Mark Landsberger and Kareem Abdul-Jabbar closed in, but Erving floated behind the basket.

**"He came on the right side and we cut him off and there was nowhere for him to go but out of bounds," said Magic Johnson. "So Julius said, 'If the only place I can go is out of bounds, then I'm going out of bounds.' So he jumped in the air out of bounds. So now here he is walking through the air. I'm thinking, 'There's**

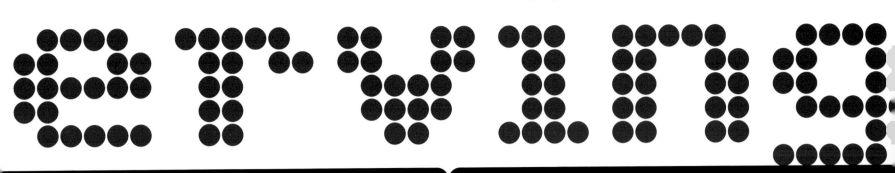

# erving

no way Doc can float all the way from this side. We got him.' I thought he was going to pass out."

Dr. J kept drifting and with the ball held firmly in his right hand, he swooped to the other side of the basket, away from Landsberger and Kareem, but still not clear of the Big Fella. **But the Doctor's afterburners had not yet ignited. When they did, he kept gliding, then fully extended his arm and the ball toward the baseline and away from the defenders.**

Kareem tried to recover, but Erving, still in flight, utilized an underhand whirlybird motion that ended with him gently releasing the ball out of his massive hand with exaggerated backspin. The ball ricocheted tenderly off the backboard, kissed the front of the rim, and dropped through the basket. The fans erupted and gave Erving a raucous ovation.

The Lakers could do nothing but admire.

**"I guess I didn't know Julius as well as I thought I did," Magic said. "I looked at [Lakers teammate Michael Cooper] and he looked at me, and I said, 'Coop, you think we should ask him to do it again?' I could not believe my eyes because of the move this man had just made. And it's still the greatest move I've ever seen in basketball, the all-time greatest."**

# AN MJ SPECTACULAR

*As basketball's ultimate hang-gliding poet, it is easy to be nonchalant when faced with the brilliance of your unique artistry.*

[ 1991 NBA Finals, Game 2
CHICAGO BULLS 107, LOS ANGELES LAKERS 86 ]
*JUNE 5, 1991*

## THE 1991 MOVE

**CD1** TRACK 22

So it was really no surprise that one day after Michael Jordan created one of pro basketball's most memorable moves — a soaring, midair, change of direction layup during Game 2 of the 1991 NBA Finals — he seemed rather blasé. "You know what?" Jordan said with a sly grin. "It wasn't even one of my best creative shots."

Well we hate to argue with a living legend, but ... Even now, more than a decade after the wondrous event, the basketball world still revels over this rare combination of sheer flight and incomprehensible creativity. In the fourth quarter of a 107-86 victory over the Los Angeles Lakers en route to his first NBA crown, Jordan took off somewhere near the free throw line in old Chicago Stadium and ended up in basketball folklore. Jordan took a pass from Cliff

Levingston and began soaring toward the hoop with the ball held well over his head, palmed firmly in his right hand. "I was definitely in a dunk mode," Jordan said. "And maybe I took off further back than I thought."

When he left the ground, it appeared to be a rocket launch that would be accentuated by a thunderous

dunk. "I saw Sam [Perkins] out of the corner of my eye and figured he was going to come over and try to block my shot," Jordan said. "So I figured, 'OK, better switch hands.'" Perkins didn't jump. But being the sort of spontaneous, improvisational guy that he was, Jordan saw no reason to spoil a perfectly spectacular tongue-wagging moment. So he simply brought the ball down, switched it into his left hand, and while everyone waited for him to fall to the earth, Jordan remained suspended in the air and flipped the ball in on the other side of the rim.

"You know, I probably had a wide-open shot, didn't I? I probably didn't even need to do that stuff at the end, huh?" Jordan said.

From such midair miscalculations, the stuff of basketball legends are made.

> "IT WASN'T EVEN ONE OF MY BEST CREATIVE SHOTS."
>
> **MICHAEL JORDAN**

61

[ **HOUSTON ROCKETS 114, LOS ANGELES LAKERS 112** ]

*MAY 21, 1986*

# IMAGINE YOURSELF IN THE WORLD OF RALPH SAMPSON ON MAY 21, 1986.

It is Game 5 of the Western Conference Finals. You are playing in the Fabulous Forum, the home of the defending NBA champion Los Angeles Lakers — the Showtime Lakers of Pat Riley, Magic Johnson, Kareem Abdul-Jabbar and James Worthy. Yet your Houston Rockets have a surprising 3-1 lead in the series.

## SAMPSON ★ TO THE RESCUE! ★

**CD1 TRACK 23**

BUZZER BEATER BOOSTS ROCKETS INTO FINALS

### This game is tied. One second is left. The ball is hurtling in your general direction.

The basket is somewhere behind your right shoulder, and seven feet, two inches of Hall of Fame purple and gold is applying pressure to your spine. While fighting off Abdul-Jabbar in the post, you must elevate your 7-foot-4 body into the air to grasp the pass from Rodney McCray. In one motion, you jump, catch, turn and shoot. You do not look good. Your knees are splayed out with your heels almost touching, not unlike a mutant ballet dancer. But it is practical. Before Abdul-Jabbar can react, the ball is caught, shot and …

### the buzzer blares.

The ball hits the front of the rim. It hangs tantalizingly in the air for a long moment before it drifts down, glances off the back rim and tumbles through the hoop. The Rockets win 114-112.

The Lakers are stunned. Their dynasty has been, at least momentarily, derailed. Their fans are silent. Your teammates are ecstatic. The Rockets are going to the Finals.

### "It's probably the best experience I've ever had in my basketball career,"

you are understating into the microphone. "It was very satisfying that I got to shoot a shot like that in a game like that."

Can you imagine it? Ralph Sampson lived it.

# BIRD IN
# FLIGHT:

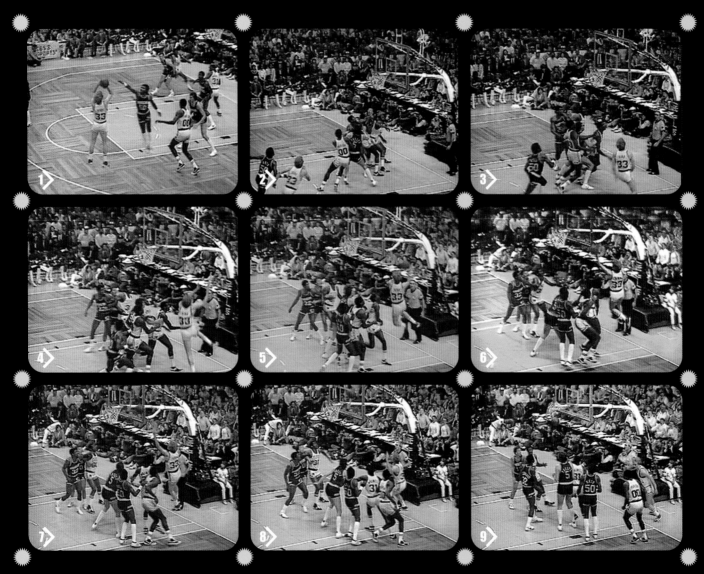

# LARRY'S LEGENDARY MOVE

1981 NBA Finals, Game 1

[ BOSTON CELTICS 98, HOUSTON ROCKETS 95 ]

*MAY 5, 1981*

**"I've never seen anything like it. It was one of the greatest plays of all time.
It was just a magnificent play."**
RED AUERBACH

# In an era when the entire game of basketball had become forever airborne, the hoop genius of Larry Bird seemed to always be defined by below-the-rim creations. Yet there is some irony here that one of the most memorable moves of his splendid Hall of Fame career was a bit of surprising, hang-gliding artistry.

The remarkable moment started out so ordinary. It was the fourth quarter of Game 1 of the 1981 NBA Finals — the first of Bird's five trips to the Finals — and Bird was on his way to a typical, all-around performance (18 points, 21 rebounds, nine assists) against the Houston Rockets. As he spotted up for a jumper to the right of the free throw line, Bird missed the shot, and it bounced high off the rim to the right side of the backboard.

Defending on the play was Houston's Robert Reid, who immediately turned toward the basket the moment the shot was released, in essence ignoring Bird and focusing in on the ball. By turning his back to Bird, Reid could not see Larry Legend go airborne … until it was too late. "I made a mistake," said Reid, who realized it, "when I saw Bird coming by my side, flying in the air."

Let's be real here. No one ever was going to mistake Bird for one of the Flying Wallendas. But the great ones often defy common wisdom when necessary. So out of necessity, Bird found his wings. While suspended in midair, he grabbed the ball with his right hand, and then sailing behind the basket, he switched it to his left hand and flipped it toward the hoop. Even for the ambidextrous Bird, who shot with his right hand and wrote with his left, it was an incredible move simply to switch hands in midair and shoot. It was all the more spectacular when it finished.

Swish!

"I've never seen anything like it," said Red Auerbach, the legendary Celtics general manager. "It was one of the greatest plays of all time. It was just a magnificent play."

# HORSING AROUND

## FREDDIE LEWIS WINS ALL-STAR MVP

### By Wayne Witt

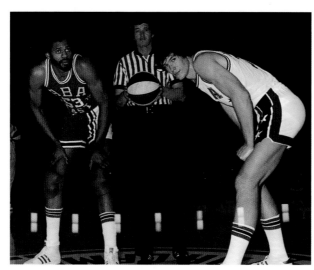

When the San Antonio Spurs were granted the 1975 ABA All-Star Game, it was a little different than the current version of NBA All-Star Games, where hundreds of people work behind the scenes to put on a weekend-long extravaganza.

I was the public relations director for the Spurs in '75, and when we first met to plan the activities for the game, we had a meeting in the kitchen of one of the guys who worked for the team. There were four people in the room. Four.

We were going to produce the All-Star Game.

Our goal was to make it as "Texas" as possible, so we corralled companies all over San Antonio and South Texas and got them to make All-Star merchandise for us. When our guests walked into the Hilton Hotel, which incidentally was the only luxury hotel downtown at the time, the consensus remark was, "How in the hell are we going to get all this stuff home?" Because the beds, tables and counters were literally covered with stuff — Lone Star beer, tortilla chips, fishing lures, cigars, sunglasses, and on and on. It was incredible.

In keeping with the Texas theme, we decided that the MVP of the game would get several items, including a Stetson and a registered quarter horse. We got the horse, whose name was Tuff Julie, and we even brought her to a couple of games, walked her around the arena and said: "This is what the MVP of the All-Star Game will get, so come and buy a ticket."

Freddie Lewis of St. Louis scored 26 points in the game, led the East to a 151-124 victory, and won the MVP award. But he was not interested in horses and had no clue what to do with Tuff Julie. He was willing to wear the Stetson, but in those days, the Afros were so big that the hat just sat on top of his head.

Lewis kept saying he didn't want the horse, so Angelo Drossos, who was our owner, told him we would sell the horse and give him the money, which was about $2,000. While there are many great moves in this chapter, Freddie's may be the best for one reason.

Two weeks later, the horse died.

FREDDIE
1975 ABA
★ ★ ★ ★
ALL-STAR GAME MVP
LEWIS

With the emergence of air travel, the Knicks annual visit to the Green Parrot Café became irrelevant as they were able to fly to Fort Wayne directly. The efficiency in travel time made for a better performance on the court.

# TRAIN TO NOWHERE
## ON THE ROAD IN THE EARLY NBA

In the early days of the NBA, teams traveled mostly by rail and played many games in small towns with great basketball tradition, but still small towns. One was Fort Wayne, Ind., which was so small that trains often would not stop. That made it a challenge for NBA teams, who sometimes traveled long distances by rail to play games on consecutive days.

**But it also made for some lively stories and great memories, including one told by legendary announcer Marty Glickman, who was the broadcaster for New York Knicks games beginning in the 1940s. This is Glickman's account of one of the more famous recurring episodes of early travel in the NBA: The Tale of the Famous Green Parrot Café.**

"Travel facilities were limited and makeshift connections were necessary. There was one trip that was almost unbelievable. The Knicks would play a Saturday night game in Rochester, N.Y., and then play the next night against the Pistons in Fort Wayne. We'd board the 20th Century Limited train at the Rochester station at midnight.

"Then at about 5 a.m., in mid-winter of course, the train would make a non-scheduled stop on an open wooden platform in the middle of an Indiana prairie. The sleepy Knicks would get off carrying their bags and the train would leave. And about a half-mile away across the prairie, in the half-light of early dawn, we'd see a small cluster of lights of a little town.

**"We'd walk to these lights to look for the Green Parrot Café. After we found it, we'd toss a few pebbles into the second floor window of the two-story building. This would wake up a woman who would open the window, look down and say,**

'Oh, the Knickerbockers. I'll be right down.' Fifteen minutes, after she'd call four or five of her friends, she'd be downstairs with her cronies, who had brought their beat-up old automobiles and the Knicks and I would pile into four or five cars and drive some 40 miles to Fort Wayne."

The next night, the game would be played, and the visitors would again depart. Getting out of Fort Wayne, however, must have been easier than getting in because there is no accompanying fable that rivals the colorful story of the Green Parrot Café.

**The Green Parrot Café always left the light on for broadcaster Marty Glickman and the New York Knicks as they made their way to Fort Wayne, Ind., in the late '40s.**

The jubilation in the stands was a perfect reflection of Shaquille O'Neal's face. The 7-foot-1, 315-pound mass of muscle was almost floating down the court with a child like, wide-eyed look of elation, pointing to the ecstatic crowd, celebrating a triumph so unlikely, and, at the moment, so sweet.

Lakers fans had waited more than a decade for a return to glory, and they thought it would arrive simultaneously with Shaq, who joined the team in 1996. But it wasn't until 2000 that they would get the one play that would epitomize what they had expected of the most dominant big man in the game.

With 40 seconds left in the fourth quarter, O'Neal climbed the upper reaches on the court at the STAPLES Center to throw down an alley-oop dunk. That put the final touches on an 89-84 series-clinching victory over the Portland Trail Blazers, sending the Lakers into their first NBA Finals in

nine years. Yet the enormity of the story was not so much that the Lakers had won, but how they had done it, rallying from a 15-point, fourth-quarter deficit to go from the verge of an embarrassing collapse to a rousing rebirth.

**"Game 7s are very interesting, but I've never seen any quite like that one before," said Lakers coach Phil Jackson, the Zen master who directed the Chicago Bulls to six titles before coming to L.A. to work his magic on Shaq & Co. and help them to realize their potential.**

For most of the year, it appeared that the Lakers were devotedly following Jackson. They had finished with the best record in the NBA at 67-15. They had marched into the Western Conference Finals on a roll, winning the semifinal series against Phoenix four games to one, then ripping off to a 3-1 series lead over Portland. Inexplicably, however, the Lakers began crumbling, losing two straight games and flirting with a three-game losing streak for the first time all season. And they were collapsing at home, where they trailed the Blazers by 15 points, 75-60, with 10:28 left in the fourth quarter.

"We were down by a lot of points, and we were shooting ourselves in the foot," said O'Neal. "Phil made a couple of comments and I pulled the guys together and said that we have come too far to blow it, so let's fight, let's claw and hit some shots."

In the final 10-plus minutes, the Lakers and Blazers reversed roles. Portland suddenly became tentative and inept. The Blazers

missed 13 consecutive shots and were 5-for-27 in the quarter. O'Neal, Brian Shaw and Kobe Bryant hit buckets. Robert Horry and Shaw fired in three-point missiles. Shaq dominated the lane defensively, knocking down a shot. With 4:02 left, Shaw tossed in another three-pointer, and the Lakers completed a 15-0 run to tie the score at 75.

The two teams traded baskets to even the game again at 79, but then the Lakers scored four straight. The Blazers were toast. Bryant helped provide the finishing touch. He drove into the lane, drew a double-team, flicked the ball up high, where, in one motion, Shaq, who finished with 18 points, nine rebounds and was 8-of-12 from the free throw line, caught it and slammed down a vicious right-handed dunk that triggered the rowdy celebration. Two weeks later, the confetti was coming down again in the STAPLES Center, where the Lakers won the NBA championship, defeating the Indiana Pacers.

"This is what makes champions," said Bryant, who had been brilliant with 25 points, 11 rebounds, seven assists and four blocked shots. "We watched Game 7s growing up all the time, and to finally play in one is a real thrill."

*"This is what makes champions. We watched Game 7s growing up all the time, and to finally play in one is a real thrill."*

**KOBE BRYANT**

# GAME 7

**25**
POINTS

**11**
REBOUNDS

**7**
ASSISTS

**4**
BLOCKS

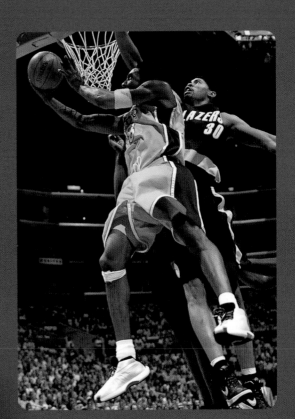

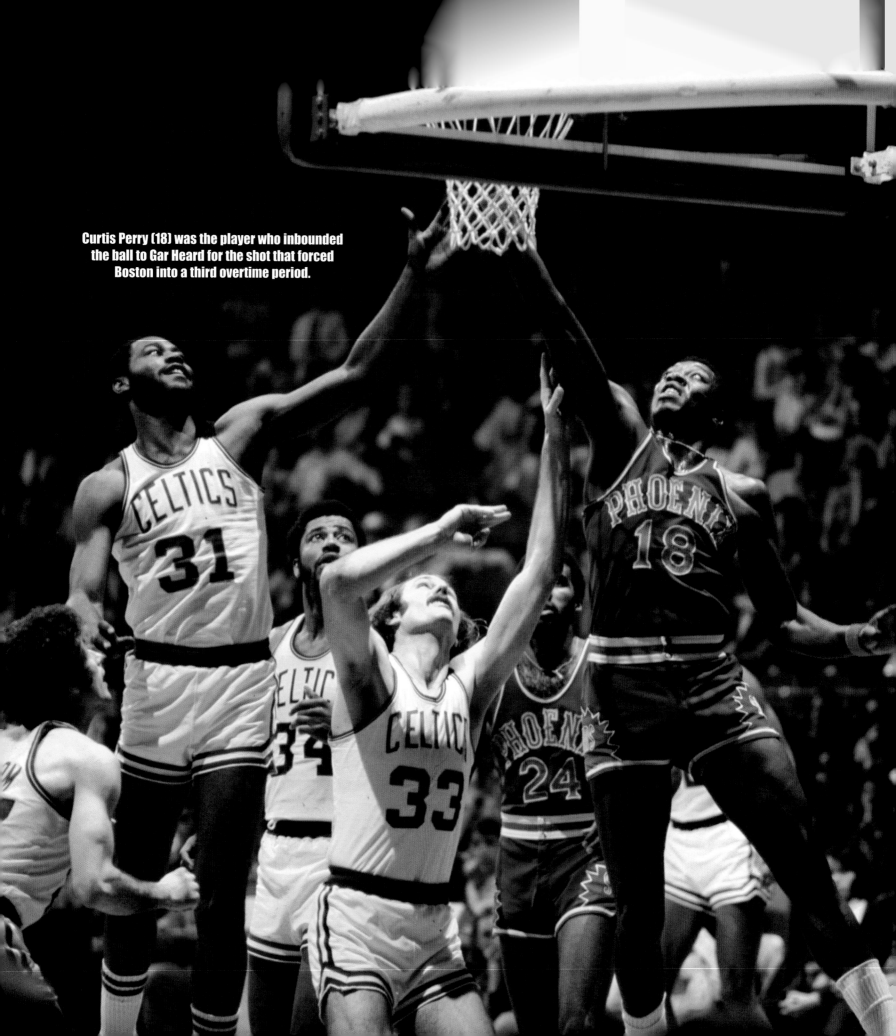

Curtis Perry (18) was the player who inbounded the ball to Gar Heard for the shot that forced Boston into a third overtime period.

DAVE COWENS

**CD1**

TRACK

**29**

1976 NBA Finals, Game 5
[ BOSTON CELTICS 128, PHOENIX SUNS 126,  3 OT ]
*June 4, 1976*

PAUL WESTPHAL

# A GARDEN
# CLASSIC

## CELTICS OUTLAST SUNS IN 3 OTS

Of all of basketball's grand galleries of hoop art, it seems quite fitting that one of the most exhilarating masterpieces in NBA Finals history occurred inside the dank, smoke-filled, championship-rich confines of the Boston Garden.

If the walls of that ancient basketball temple could talk, there is no doubt they would rank Game 5 of the 1976 NBA Finals between the hometown Celtics and the Phoenix Suns as an all-time keeper, which is quite lofty considering this is the franchise of Bill Russell, who had retired seven years earlier. The Celtics were no longer a dynasty, but led by fiery redhead Dave Cowens, they still had managed to be in the position of winning their second title in three years.

Boston — with the league's second-best record — rode into the Finals as the heavy favorite over the surprising Suns, who fin-

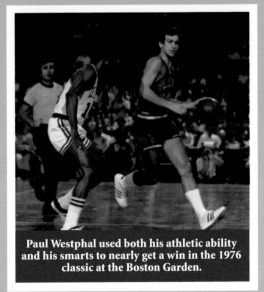

**Paul Westphal used both his athletic ability and his smarts to nearly get a win in the 1976 classic at the Boston Garden.**

ished the regular season with a mediocre 42-40 record before running off a string of postseason upsets to face the powerful Celtics. The series had gone back and forth, with the Celtics taking the first two games at Boston, and Phoenix coming back to win Games 3 and 4. But as the series returned beneath the rumbling trains of old North Station, no one could have imagined what was about to occur on the Garden's sacred parquet floor.

Boston had raced out to a 20-point lead nine minutes into the first quarter, and the 15,320 rowdy hometown fans believed this pivotal game was going to be over quickly. But then Paul Westphal, Phoenix's stylish guard, rallied the Suns in the fourth quarter, and the drama began.

With less than 90 seconds left, Westphal hit a spinning, fade-away jumper to cut Boston's lead to 94-91. A few seconds later, he tipped the ball away from Jo Jo White and immediately raced down the floor. Teammate Alvan Adams picked up the ball, threw a length-of-the-court pass to Westphal, who made a layup and was fouled by Charlie Scott. With only 39 seconds left in regulation, the former Celtic drained the free throw. Score tied at 94-all.

The game would go into overtime when the two teams traded free throws in the final seconds of regulation. But the drama had barely begun.

There would be one overtime, then another, and the rumble inside the Garden grew. The mood had gone from utter joy to nervous desperation, as the crowd began to wonder if disaster was coming. But with 10 seconds left in the second overtime, Boston led 109-106 and the crowd was energized again, preparing for a raucous celebration. Then Dick Van Arsdale hit an 18-footer with 15 seconds left and Westphal stole another inbounds

pass and fed it to Curtis Perry, who shot and missed. But Perry grabbed the ball when it tipped off the hands of Havlicek and before any Boston player could react, Perry then drained a jumper from 16 feet. Only five seconds left. Suddenly, it was Phoenix in the lead, 110-109, and it was the Celtics who were looking for miracles.

Don Nelson inbounded the ball at half court to Havlicek, who took three dribbles to his left, then hit a leaping, leaning jumper.

"The ballgame is over!! John Havlicek won it!!" shouted CBS's Brent Musburger.

On the Garden scoreboard, and even

...plays the peacemaker as Celtics' Dave Cowens makes menacing gestures at Suns' Curtis Perry. Powers, fan were in altercation at end of 2d OT. (Bill Brett photo)

# Celtics win, 128-126—in triple OT

Dick Van Arsdale's 18-footer with 15 seconds remaining in the second overtime cut Boston's lead to 109-108.

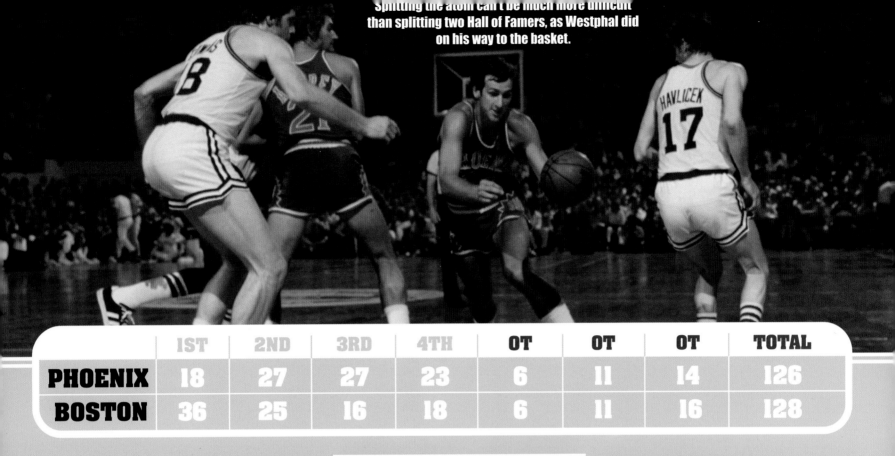

|  | 1ST | 2ND | 3RD | 4TH | OT | OT | OT | TOTAL |
|---|---|---|---|---|---|---|---|---|
| **PHOENIX** | 18 | 27 | 27 | 23 | 6 | 11 | 14 | 126 |
| **BOSTON** | 36 | 25 | 16 | 18 | 6 | 11 | 16 | 128 |

on CBS, the words were flashed: "Boston 111, Phoenix 110. Final score." As the Celtics raced off the floor into their locker room, Garden fans spilled onto the court in a mad celebration. It was a rowdy but joyful mob until the fans learned that head referee Richie Powers ruled that the game was not officially over. Havlicek's shot went through the hoop with at least one second on the clock, so Powers ordered the game clock reset to one second. A mob scene erupted on the floor, and one out-of-control spectator attacked Powers. With order finally restored and both teams back on the court, Westphal made a brilliant suggestion to head coach John MacLeod. The Suns were all out of timeouts, and had to take the ball out of bounds under the Boston basket. With only one second left, it was too far to go to get a decent shot. But Westphal told MacLeod to call the timeout anyway to draw a technical foul.

"I asked Richie Powers if we called the timeout, if we could still advance the ball to halfcourt," Westphal said. Powers said yes. So the Suns called the illegal timeout, Boston's Jo Jo White sank the technical shot to give Boston a 112-110 lead and

**"The ballgame is over!! John Havlicek won it!!"**

BRENT MUSBURGER

Phoenix got the ball back at halfcourt in a better position to get off a decent — albeit miracle — shot. As the teams came out for the final second of play, Perry inbounded the ball from half court, and Musburger made the call:

"Gar Heard turnaround shot in the air…AAAAAHHHHHH….IT'S GOOD!! IT'S TIED AGAIN! I DON'T BELIEVE IT!!!"

The Suns had climbed out of the grave again. Triple overtime.

"It was like a miracle. Something that happened and I was stunned," Heard said. "I was stunned until the next day."

In the third OT, the Celtics held a six-point lead with 36 seconds left, but the Suns would not die. After Westphal sank two free throws to cut the lead to 128-126 in the final seconds, he almost came up with another miracle. He barely missed stealing another Boston pass along the sideline. White, however, beat him to the ball, and the clock finally ran out on the Suns' miracles. But not until the team that was only two games better than .500 in the regular season had starred in one of the greatest games in NBA Finals history.

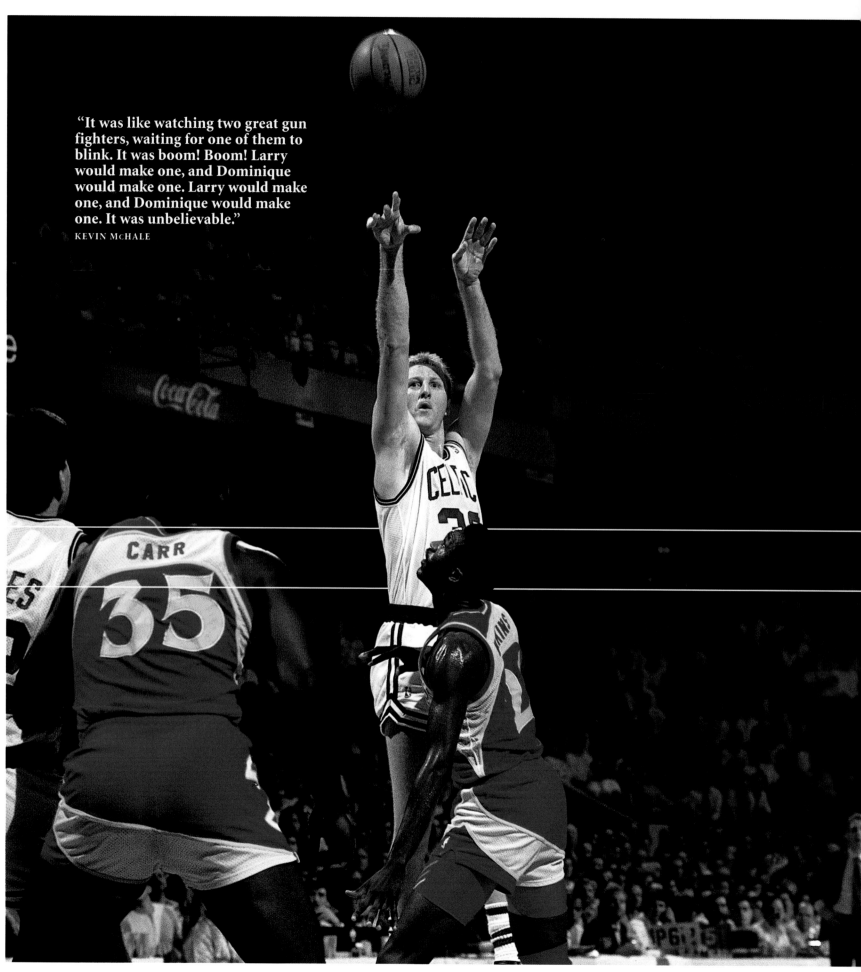

"It was like watching two great gun fighters, waiting for one of them to blink. It was boom! Boom! Larry would make one, and Dominique would make one. Larry would make one, and Dominique would make one. It was unbelievable."

KEVIN McHALE

**CD1**
TRACK
**30**

1988 NBA Eastern Conference Semifinals, Game 7
[ BOSTON CELTICS 118, ATLANTA HAWKS 116 ]
*MAY 22, 1988*

# CLASH OF THE
# TITANS

## BIRD vs. WILKINS IN GAME 7 CLASSIC

For 12 transcendent minutes of Game 7 of the 1988 NBA Eastern Conference semifinals, Larry Bird and Dominique Wilkins combined for one of those rare moments of shared creative genius. It was like Fred Astaire in a tap duel with Savion Glover, or Jimi Hendrix trading hot guitar licks with B.B. King. It was an incandescent duel of contrasting basketball styles that produced one of the most substantive individual postseason duels in NBA history.

# WILKINS

There was Boston's Bird, a master of below-the-rim excellence. In stark contrast, there was Atlanta's Wilkins, nicknamed rather appropriately the "Human Highlight Film." While Bird was an earthbound man of hoop nuance, Wilkins was an explosive pogo-stick, a slashing, high-rising frequent flier.

It was during this breathless fourth quarter of this game eventually won by Boston 118-116, that Bird and Wilkins would share one common bond: They were fearless superstars who elevated their games to unconscious brilliance as their teams battled in a decisive seventh game showdown. With everything on the line, and most of the basketball world watching, these two future Hall of Famers waged a glorious war — Bird firing nervelessly from below the rim, Wilkins weaving his magnificence on a high wire.

In perhaps his finest moment as a pro, Wilkins scored 47 points, including 16 in the fourth quarter on a collection of in-your-face jumpers and levitation-act drives to the hoop. Yet whatever Wilkins dished out, Bird topped when the game was on the line. The 6-foot-9-inch forward was utterly magnificent, scoring 20 of his 34 points in the fourth. He hit on nine of 10 shots, each one more significant than the other.

**"It was like watching two great gun fighters, waiting for one of them to blink,"** said Celtics forward Kevin McHale. **"It was boom! Boom! Larry would make one, and Dominique would make one. Larry would make one, and Dominique would make one. It was unbelievable. I tell you there was one four-minute stretch there that was as pure a form of basketball as you're ever going to see."**

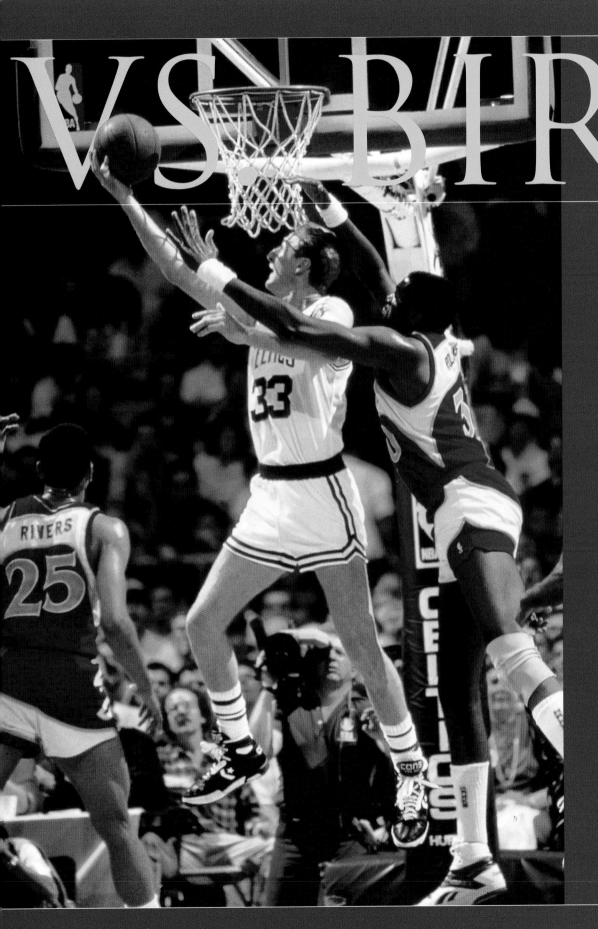

# VS. BIRD

McHale (33 points, with 21 of those and nine rebounds in the first half) and Atlanta's Doc Rivers (12 assists, 10 points in the first half), had climbed up on that narrow ledge with Bird and Wilkins before intermission. But as the game wound down to the critical final moments, there was no one sharing the plateau. It was all Bird and Dominique.

The last two minutes were classic. Bird made a three-point jumper with 1:43 left, then a driving layup with 26 seconds left for a 114-109 Boston lead. Dominique came right back with a rebound of his own missed shot. His basket made it 114-111.

Then Bird made the biggest play of the game — the sort of play that was his signature. Nothing spectacular. Nothing fancy. Just smart, clear thinking and timely. As soon as Wilkins' shot went through the net, Bird grabbed it, stepped out of bounds and fired a pass to a wide-open Danny Ainge, who was at half court. Ainge quickly raced to the Boston basket for a layup that missed, but was called good when Rivers was whistled for goaltending. With 17 seconds to go, it was Boston, 116-111, and this marvelous hoop battle had come to an end.

"That was the greatest performance I've ever witnessed," Celtics guard Dirk Minniefield said of Bird's show. "It was like he was playing on Mt. Olympus and we were all down on the Greek islands."

With one exception: Wilkins had been up there with Bird on Olympus all day.

**"A lot of games you wonder what more you could have done," said Wilkins. "But not today. I can honestly say I did everything I could. We all did."**

# SHOW AT THE JOE:
# KING•V

*Bernard King scored 44 points and had 12 rebounds — despite playing with the flu and splints on each of his middle fingers because they were dislocated.*

1984 Eastern Conference First Round, Game 5
## [ NEW YORK KNICKS 127, DETROIT PISTONS 123 (OT) ]
*APRIL 27, 1984*

**F**irst-round playoff matchups often serve as mere tune-ups. The higher seeded team makes its way through the championship bracket, the underdog goes gently into the night and the basketball world is on its proper axis.

By the evening of April 27, 1984, however, the New York Knicks and Detroit Pistons had created something special in their first-round Eastern Conference series. It was almost as if they had begun with their backs touching, walked 10 paces toward their respective baskets, then turned to fire shot after dramatic shot at each other.

**That the Knicks were even able to survive in the oppressive heat of Joe Lewis Arena much less win 127-123 in overtime was a credit to Bernard King, who scored 44 points and had 12 rebounds — despite playing with the flu *and* splints on each of his middle fingers because they were dislocated.**

That the game even went into overtime was a credit to Isiah Thomas, who pierced the Knicks defense for 16 consecutive points in a period of 1:33 at the end of regulation.

The combination was a basketball duel of the ages.

"Never have I ever been involved in something like this," said Knicks coach Hubie Brown. Neither had any of the 21,208 drained, dazzled and dazed fans.

**To begin with, it was unseasonably warm in Detroit. Add to that, the air**

**conditioning in the building had stopped working. The Joe had turned into a sauna bath. "It was at least 120 degrees in there," said Brown, exaggerating only slightly.**

The stifling heat made life particularly rough for King, who had terrorized Detroit's defenders all series, averaging 42.6 points in the first four games. But he somehow fought through it all — the heat, the flu, the splints and the grueling series. After a Louis Orr miss, King brought the duel to a conclusion with a swooping slam dunk over four Pistons and two of his own teammates. That effectively put the game out of reach. "He looked like Superman on that one," said Knicks guard Trent Tucker.

So did Thomas, who had 35 points in a display of cold-blooded three-pointers and cat-like-quick slashes to the basket, but was left with the pain of defeat . . . and the respect of the victors. Brown paid proper tribute saying, "Isiah Thomas put on one of the greatest shows ever seen in the NBA."

S.ISIAH

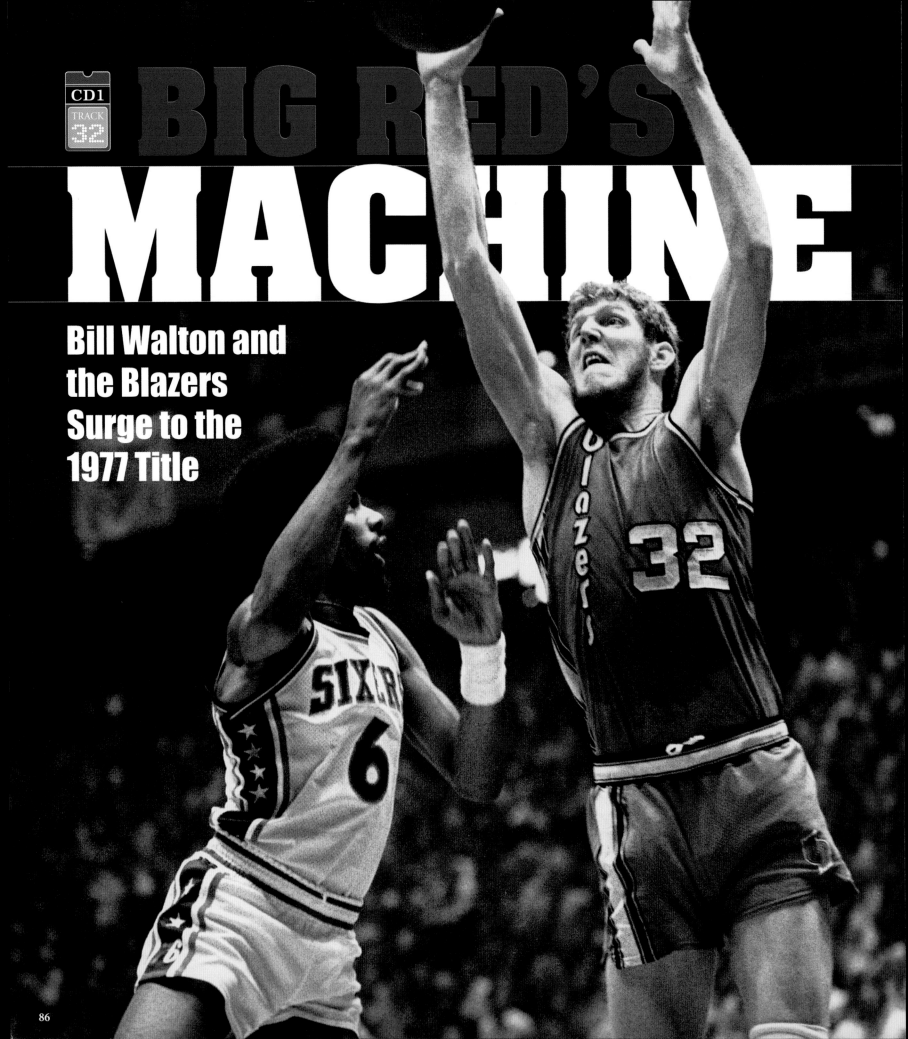

# BIG RED'S
# MACHINE

**Bill Walton and the Blazers Surge to the 1977 Title**

As the 1977 NBA Finals unfolded, there was one steady theme running throughout the fascinating conflict between the Western Conference champion Portland Trail Blazers and the Eastern Conference's Philadelphia 76ers.

# Could the sway of Portland's team-oriented concept overcome the individual power of Philly's band of dazzling All-Stars?

In basketball circles, this was a morality play of sorts, a clash of modern hoop style against traditional basketball substance.

The athletic grace and power of Julius Erving often resulted in easy dunks.

Block Party: Bill Walton was a defensive force throughout the series, routinely swatting shots such as this one from Steve Mix.

The Sixers were heavily favored, with an All-Star roster heavy with the likes of **Julius Erving, George McGinnis** and **Doug Collins**, plus the outrageous youngsters **World B. Free, Joe "Jelly Bean" Bryant** and **Darryl Dawkins**, who were aching to be stars. On the other side were the Blazers, anchored by the gifted center **Bill Walton** (18.6 points, league-leading 14.4 rebounds and 3.25 blocked shots) and enforcer power forward **Maurice Lucas**, who led the team in scoring with a 20.2-point average. Walton and Lucas carried the load inside, but they were surrounded by a perfect complement of perimeter players — **Lionel Hollins, Bob Gross, Johnny Davis, Dave Twardzik, Larry Steele** and **Herm Gilliam**.

The Sixers took a quick 2-0 lead in the series, but as the teams traveled back to Portland, everything changed. In Portland, the Blazers found their running game, stifled Philly's vaunted attack and frustrated and confused the overconfident Sixers. **After back-to-back victories at home by 22 and 32 points, the Blazers then won Game 5 in Philly, setting up the thrilling sixth game in Portland and providing the stage for Walton to take over.**

And he did, scoring 20 points, pulling down 23 rebounds, dishing seven assists and blocking an NBA Finals-record eight shots in a 109-107 Blazers victory.

As the team celebrated its championship the next day with a huge parade and outdoor celebration downtown, Walton gave a memorable speech. He thanked the fans for their support, then asked the guy who stole his bike to please return it and then poured beer over Mayor Neil Goldschmidt's head. Amazingly, the thief actually did return the bike, proving, at the very end, that sometimes even a talented individual can become a part of the team.

Philly's George McGinnis didn't find a whole lot of daylight throughout the series thanks to the stifling defense of Maurice Lucas and his Blazer teammates.

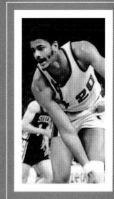

# MAURICE LUCAS:
## Blazing A Championship Trail

### By Bill Walton

The turning point in our 1977 series occurred with five minutes left in Game 2 when Maurice Lucas stood up and challenged Philadelphia's big bully Darryl Dawkins. The Sixers were on their way to a commanding 2-0 series lead when Dawkins threw a roundhouse punch at our teammate Bob Gross after they had battled for a loose ball. It turned out to be a disastrous mistake. An enraged Maurice responded and the series was never the same. Both benches cleared but Maurice's message was undeniably clear: **Don't ever mess with any of my teammates again.**

When the series shifted to Portland, we knew it was over for Philadelphia. Even though we were down 0-2, the outpouring of love we received from the Blazermaniacs that jammed the Memorial Coliseum prior to tipoff lifted us to a higher level. When Maurice's name was called during pregame introductions, he jogged to the Philly bench to make peace. He shook Darryl's hand and defused an extremely volatile situation. Dawkins was shocked by this demonstration of sportsmanship and turned into a big sissy for the remainder of the series.

Maurice went on to dominate Game 3 with a 27-point, 12-rebound performance. He intimidated and devastated his opponent, George McGinnis, grounding this high-scoring forward throughout the series. Maurice's performance set the tone for four straight wins.

While I was voted the Finals MVP, Maurice's toughness, leadership and commitment to the team in that series are the reasons the championship banner hangs in Portland.

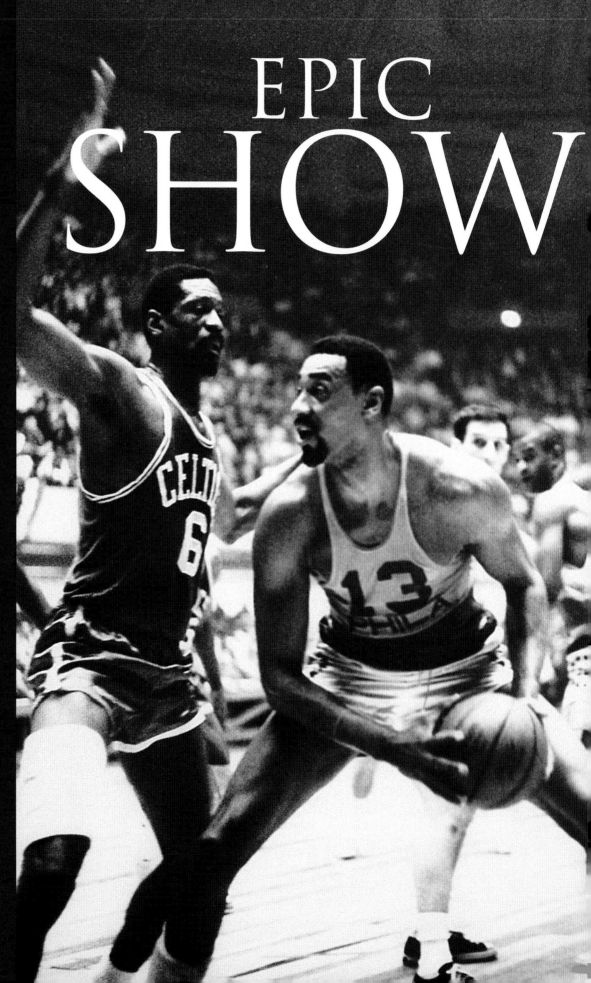

# WILT

# EPIC SHOW

Wilt Chamberlain entered the NBA as a man who would be king. His legend began in high school in Philadelphia and grew every year. He was the prototypical man among boys and by the time he reached the NBA, he was larger than life. Even more ominous for NBA teams, however, was that he seemed bigger than the league, ready to dominate in a way that was completely unprecedented.

Before his coronation could become official, however, he did have to unseat the reigning champion, one William Felton Russell. In each of Russell's first three seasons in Boston, he had led the Celtics to the Finals. And he had won two championships.

While Chamberlain was physically overpowering, Russell had a competitive fire that raged, but not out of control. He was the NBA's basketball valedictorian, a man of immense intelligence and mental strength with exquisite skills that were channeled relentlessly in one direction — winning.

Chamberlain elicited the greatest performances of Russell's Hall of Fame career, but it was almost self-defense. Anyone incapable of responding to the physical challenge of Wilt quickly wilted. Russell did it with guile, with finesse, with tenacity, and with a healthy dose of fear.

"After I played him for the first time," Russell said, "I said: 'Let's see.

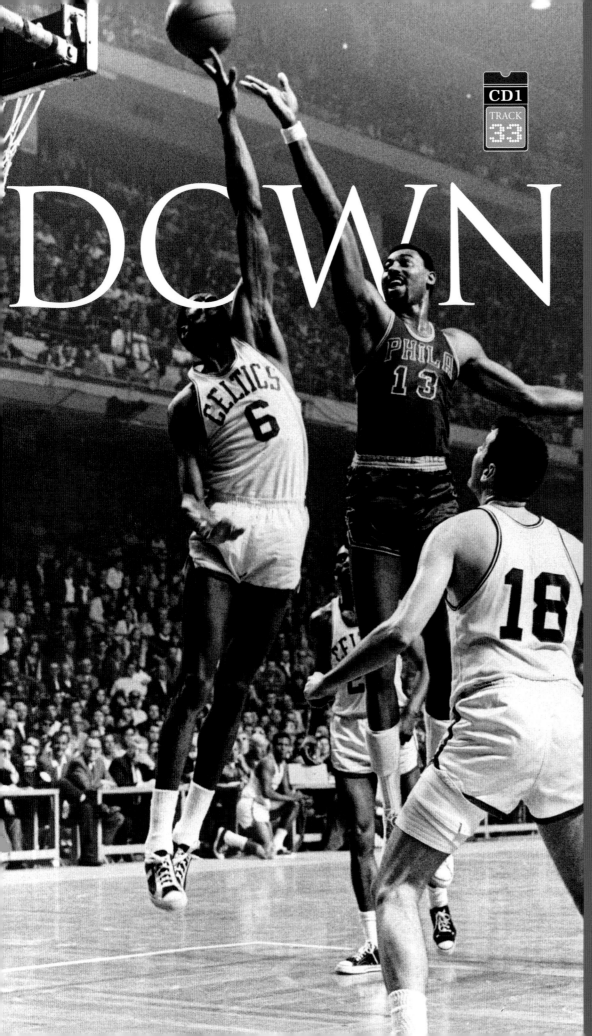

# DOWN

# RUSSELL

He's four or five inches taller. He's 40 or 50 pounds heavier. His vertical leap is at least as good as mine. He can get up and down the floor as well as I can. And he's smart. The real problem with all this is I have to show up!'"

But show up he did, and often with a supporting cast that was far superior to Wilt's. It may not have mattered, however, because if Bill Russell established anything during his career, it was that he was the greatest competitor and winner in NBA history. The Wilt-Russell clashes were masterpieces, but in the end, it was a classic case of one winning many battles, and the other winning the war.

Consider the statistics in games they played against each other:

SCORING AVERAGE:
Chamberlain . . . . . . . . . 28.7
Russell . . . . . . . . . . . . . . 14.5

REBOUNDING AVERAGE:
Chamberlain . . . . . . . . . 28.7
Russell . . . . . . . . . . . . . . 23.7

VICTORIES:
Russell . . . . . . . . . . . . . . . . 85
Chamberlain . . . . . . . . . . . 57

But there was even a more important statistic:

CHAMPIONSHIPS:
Russell . . . . . . . . . . . . . . . . 11
Chamberlain . . . . . . . . . . . 2

*The last time the two players met was in 1969, more than three decades ago.
Yet basketball still savors them as if the final meeting was yesterday. When they first began
playing against each other, the NBA consisted of only eight teams. So familiarity helped create
a rivalry that has never been matched. The 142 times Russell and Chamberlain
played against each other is easily an NBA record.*

**"We were forced to play against the Celtics 11 to 13 times during the regular season,"
recalled Chamberlain. "And if you think that wasn't enough, then we had another
seven games against them in the playoffs, if it went seven games. So I had a
chance to see William Felton Russell much more than I wanted to."**

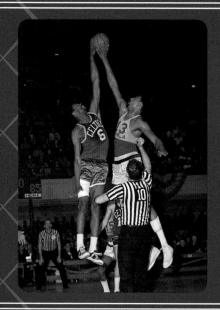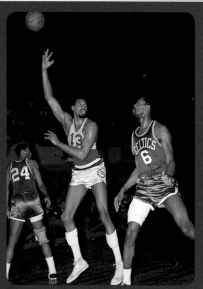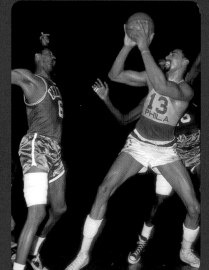

The public, of course, disagreed. Russell-Chamberlain battles were highly anticipated events, many of them coming on Sunday afternoons on national television. Although the press and fans thought of the two as rivals, they actually were very friendly with one another. During the NBA at 50 celebration, in fact, Russell revealed that they often had dinner together before games.

"I had Thanksgiving dinner with my friend Wilt six years in a row, with him and his family in Philadelphia," Russell said. "The competition between us was really difficult. He treated me to dinner and then tried to beat the hell out of me. And I tried to reciprocate when he came to Boston."

Their skills were, of course, very different. Chamberlain was all power with a superior offensive skill that enabled him to average more than 50 points a game one season. Russell was a defensive genius who had a unique approach to his specialty of blocking shots. Unlike many players who swat shots into the stands, Russell would merely redirect the shot, often flicking it out to a teammate to start a fast break. No one in the history of the game has come even remotely close to matching Russell's artistic approach to shot blocking.

As different as they were, however, they also were very much alike. Both were great athletes, once challenging each other in the decathlon. Their similarities are perhaps best demonstrated by their common rebounding skill. In NBA history, players

have had 40 or more rebounds 24 times. Of those 24, Chamberlain (14) and Russell (eight) combined for 22. In fact, Chamberlain's most dominant performance may not have been his 100-point game but his 55-rebound game that came at Russell's expense. As was the case more often than not, however, Russell's team won that game 132-129.

"People say it was the greatest individual rivalry they've ever seen," Russell said. "I agree with that. Let me assure you that if either Wilt's or Russ' coach had ever told one of them he couldn't guard the other guy, he would have lost that player forever."

Each relished the matchup, but no more so than the public. And no more so than history.

> "Bill Russell helped make my dream a better dream because when you play with the best, you know you have to play your best."
>
> WILT CHAMBERLAIN

## THE MATCHUP: GAMES vs. EACH OTHER

| | GAMES | POINTS | AVERAGE | REBOUNDS | REB AVG |
|---|---|---|---|---|---|
| Chamberlain | 142 | 4077 | 28.7 | 4072 | 28.7 |
| Russell | 142 | 2060 | 14.5 | 3373 | 23.7 |

CHAMPIONSHIPS

**RUSSELL 11     CHAMBERLAIN 2**

> "People say it was the greatest individual rivalry they've ever seen. I agree with that. Let me assure you that if either Wilt's or Russ' coach had ever told one of them he couldn't guard the other guy, he would have lost that player forever."
>
> BILL RUSSELL

# CELTICS

## THE RIVALRY THAT WAS NOT

# LAKERS

Despite heroic efforts by Jerry West (44), time and again the Celtics, led by Hall of Famers such as John Havlicek (17) and Bill Russell (6), outlasted the Lakers and won the ultimate game.

**Satch Sanders (16) and Jerry West pursue the ball.**

If a rivalry supposes an inherent give-and-take between two teams, can the Lakers-Celtics battles of the late '50s and '60s be considered one? A rivalry defined would be something along the lines of Ali-Frazier. Two victories for Ali; one for Frazier. Each a classic.

From 1958-59 — the Lakers' penultimate season in Minneapolis — to 1968-69, the Lakers and Celtics met a remarkable seven times in the NBA Finals. In those series, there was one sweep; one series went five games; two went six games; and three went the distance. In what seems to defy logic, the Celtics won every series.

A perfect seven-for-seven.

Where, some may ask, is the rivalry if one team builds a dynasty on the ruins of an organization that seems to always be second best? Year after year, the Lakers would win 50 or more games and dispatch all Western Division challengers only to play bridesmaid to the Bill Russell-led Celtics.

"If we played Boston four on four, without Russell, we probably would have won every series," said Hot Rod Hundley, who played for three of those losing Laker teams. "The guy killed us. He's the one who prevented us from achieving true greatness."

It was the ultimate heart breaker for the Lakers, who were unquestionably a great team, just never were able to win the last game of the year against Boston. Still, the competition between the two teams was marvelous and memorable.

John Havlicek won his first title in his rookie year in 1963 when the Celtics upended Los Angeles. He would help beat the Lakers four other times in the '60s.

**1959**

## Celtics 4, Lakers 0

The Celtics had the league's best record at 52-20. The Lakers were 33-39, but upset St. Louis in the Western Division Finals. Despite keeping it close — the Lakers lost Games 1 and 4 by a total of eight points — Boston completed a sweep. The rivalry was beginning.

**1962**

## Celtics 4, Lakers 3

When Lakers guard Frank Selvy was in college at Furman, he scored 100 points in a game. He was a reliable pro; a good shooter. With five seconds left in Game 7, Selvy had an open eight-footer. He missed. Bill Russell grabbed his 40th rebound of the game. The Celtics won in overtime.

**1963**

## Celtics 4, Lakers 2

Despite four straight titles, Boston was viewed as an aging team. Bob Cousy announced that he would retire after the season. But the Celtics won a league-best 58 games and took a 2-0 series lead over the Lakers. L.A. won two of the next three, but Boston won Game 6 112-109 in L.A. Cousy dribbled out the last seconds of his Boston career and then threw the ball high in the air.

**1965**

## Celtics 4, Lakers 1

The Celtics broke their own record with 62 regular-season wins, but struggled to beat Philadelphia and Wilt Chamberlain in the Eastern Division Finals, winning Game 7 after "Havlicek stole the ball!" Boston carried that momentum to the series victory against the Lakers, who were without injured star Elgin Baylor.

**1966**

## Celtics 4, Lakers 3

The Lakers opened with an overtime victory in Boston Garden, but afterward, Red Auerbach — always the master manipulator — who had announced earlier in the season that he would retire after the playoffs, announced that Russell would be taking his place as head coach next season, the first African-American coach in NBA history. The Celtics were inspired and, despite the Game 1 victory, the Lakers were deflated and went on to lose, again.

**1968**

## Celtics 4, Lakers 2

Philadelphia interrupted Boston's dynasty the previous season, but the Celtics came back with a vengeance and upended Philadelphia in the Eastern Division Finals 4-3. The Lakers, who had rooted for Boston, thinking an aging Russell would be easier to beat than Chamberlain, got what they wished for. And Russell won his 10th title and first as coach.

**1969**

## Celtics 4, Lakers 3

The Lakers had more regular-season victories, 55 to the Celtics' 48; they finally had an inside presence having traded for Wilt Chamberlain; and they were confident going into these Finals. So much so that owner Jack Kent Cooke ordered thousands of balloons suspended in the Forum rafters for Game 7, to be released when the Lakers won. The Celtics, however, were inspired by the insult and went on to a 108-106 victory in Russell's final game. The balloons were donated to a children's hospital.

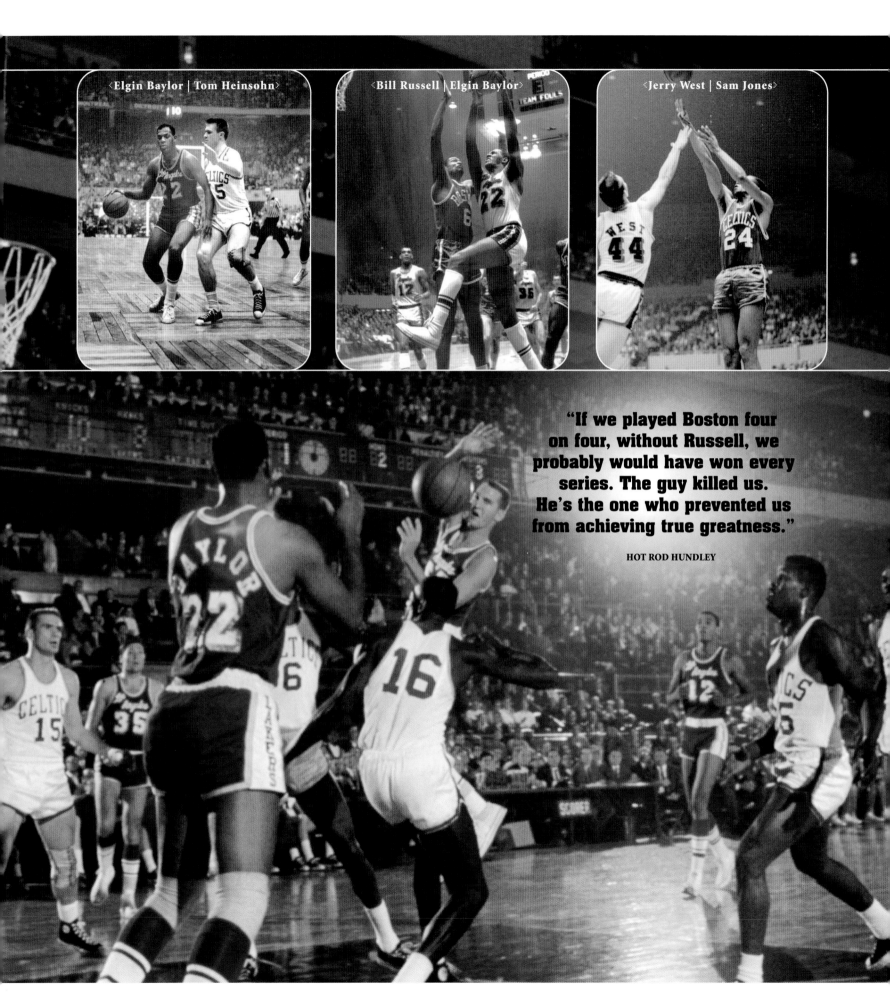

‹Elgin Baylor | Tom Heinsohn›

‹Bill Russell | Elgin Baylor›

‹Jerry West | Sam Jones›

"If we played Boston four on four, without Russell, we probably would have won every series. The guy killed us. He's the one who prevented us from achieving true greatness."

**HOT ROD HUNDLEY**

# MIAMI BLUES

## ALLAN HOUSTON SINKS THE HEAT

*Sometimes the difference between thrilling victory and excruciating defeat
is encapsulated into tiny units of time. For New York and Miami, whose young but
intense rivalry already had accounted for more than a few memorable moments,
that unit was less than a second on May 16, 1999, when the Knicks'
Allan Houston ended the Heat's season on a 10-foot runner.*

"We've lost a lot of games on last-second shots. It was finally sweet to be reversed, where we would finally win one."

PATRICK EWING

**P**laying at home and seeded No. 1, the Heat led by seven points with 9:56 left in Game 5 of the first-round series. But Miami's lead withered, and with the Heat clinging to a one-point advantage, the Knicks called timeout with 19.9 seconds left. Latrell Sprewell had the ball and the opportunity for the go-ahead shot, but Miami's Terry Porter poked the ball out of bounds with 4.5 seconds, allowing the Knicks to run a set play.

Houston had started with a dismal 1-for-7 shooting performance, but vindication awaited. After the Knicks inbounded the ball, Houston found a narrow opening between Dan Majerle and Tim Hardaway. He slithered through, elevated and released a short jumper on the move. The ball hit the rim, then the backboard, and "hung in the air for what seemed like two minutes instead of two seconds," Houston later recalled. Finally, it dropped through the net, drooping the Heat players and their fans.

**"It was definitely the biggest shot I've ever made," Houston said after the 78-77 victory. "I hit a game-winning basket in college, but to come through and take advantage of this opportunity is just a wonderful feeling."**

For the Heat, which had lost in the first round of the playoffs to the Knicks for the second straight year, it marked the third time in four seasons that the team would exit the playoffs in the first round.

**"It's one of the worst feelings I've experienced — indescribable," said P.J. Brown. "Our dreams have been dashed."**

And for Heat coach Pat Riley, whose approach to the game has always been embodied in a saying he coined — "There's winning … and there's misery." — it was even worse. "Obviously, it's very, very painful," Riley said. "This hurts a hell of a lot more than last year."

*"Obviously, it's very, very painful. This hurts a hell of a lot more than last year."*

**PAT RILEY**

## If ever there was a moment that could forever capture the sheer unexpected joy of an upset victory, this is it.

*Wrap it up and put it in an everlasting frame. Dikembe Mutombo, all 7-feet-2-inches of him, flat on his back in the middle of the court at the Seattle Coliseum, clutching a basketball high above his head, his face all lit up with the most irrepressible delirium a man could express. His tears mixed freely with his perspiration; his laughter blended together with deep, heartfelt sobs.*

This was the indelible portrait of ecstasy, captured in the electrifying moments after the buzzer had sounded to end the final game of the 1994 first-round Western Conference series between Mutombo's Denver Nuggets and the Seattle SuperSonics. The Nuggets, seeded eighth, had provoked this madness by knocking off the top-seeded Sonics 98-94 in overtime in the series-clinching fifth game. It was one of the biggest upsets in NBA playoff history.

There were so many reasons why even the most loyal Nuggets believer could not have predicted this. It was an astonishing accomplishment for the young team, which became the first No. 8 seed to knock off a No. 1 seed in the first round since the NBA went to the 16-team playoff format in 1984. Seattle posted the best record in the league in 1993-94 at 63-19, including a 37-4 record at the Coliseum. They had the All-Stars in Shawn Kemp and Gary Payton. And the experience with

Detlef Schrempf, Kendall Gill, Ricky Pierce, Sam Perkins, Nate McMillan and Michael Cage. Seattle had the home-court advantage. They also had a 2-0 lead in the series.

In contrast, Denver, which had finished with a 42-40 regular-season mark, was an inexperienced squad. Only two players on

the roster had more than four years in the NBA. There is no other way to put this: The SuperSonics were not supposed to lose to the Nuggets.

The Sonics almost lost it in regulation, but Gill came roaring down the lane and put back Payton's errant shot with five-tenths of a second left to tie it at 88 and send it into overtime. In the extra period, reserve guard Robert Pack wore out the Sonics. Put in the game because starting guard Mahmoud Abdul-Rauf was in a shooting slump, Pack scored 19 of his game-high 23 points in the second half and overtime. He made three 3-point baskets, and it was his two free throws with 18.7 seconds remaining in overtime that put Denver ahead by four and iced the victory.

History said it was impossible, particularly when the Sonics won the first two games of the series. "But who cares about history," said Pack. "History can't make me feel any better than I already feel."

# Nuggets Strike

# Gold

## Powerful SuperSonics Grounded

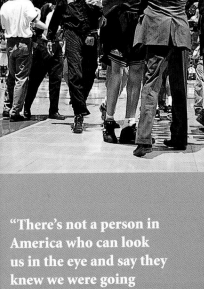

CD2

TRACK
2

1994 Western Conference First Round, Game 5

DENVER NUGGETS 98,
SEATTLE SUPERSONICS 94 (OT)

*MAY 7, 1994*

GERVIN'S 63 BEATS

THE ICEMAN COMETH

CD2
TRACK
3

# THOMPSON'S 73

**Louie hits 15,000th, Gervin wins NBA title**

**Playoffs**

Milwaukee plays at Phoenix Tuesday night in the Western Conference series opener. Los Angeles is at Seattle Wednesday night.

Eastern Conference playoffs start Wednesday night with Atlanta at Washington. Cleveland is at New York Friday night.

**DAMPIER**

**GERVIN**

**Spur special**

Copies of the special souvenir section on the San Antonio Spurs, featuring an autographed color team picture, are available in the lobby of the Express-News this week.

The section, which was inserted in last Sunday's Express-News, is being sold for 35 cents as long as the supply lasts.

It was a shootout at 1,000 paces, although in this case, it was miles and not steps. One thousand miles is the approximate distance between Detroit and New Orleans, where two of the most entertaining players in the history of basketball engaged in one of the most compelling duels ever held in different arenas.

Before games of April 9, 1978, the race for the scoring championship looked like this:

George Gervin, 81 games, 2,169 points, average of 26.78 per game.

David Thompson, 79 games, 2,099 points, average of 26.57 per game.

The Denver Nuggets were in Detroit. Thompson was in The Zone. He scored 73 points.

Reporters quickly called Gervin in his

## 27.22PPG

to get the scoring title.'"

Thompson: "After I scored the 73 points, we flew back to Denver. I started listening to the Spurs game. Wilt Chamberlain had set the record for points in one quarter with 31 and it lasted for many years. But my record of 32 points lasted for a few hours, because George scored 33 in the second quarter. By halftime George had scored 53 points. I just turned it off, knowing he would win."

Gervin: "When I got my 59th point, Doug took me out. But I went up to him a few minutes later and said, 'Just in case someone made a mistake, maybe I better go back in.' So I went back in and got four more points for my 63. That was the most memorable game I had."

# IT WAS THE CLOSEST SCORING RACE IN NBA HISTORY

## 27.15PPG

hotel room in New Orleans and told him. But Gervin wasn't called the Iceman for nothing. He shrugged his shoulders, figured he had lost the race to a talented man, and prepared for the game that night. He needed 58 points to pass Thompson. He got 63.

The two have reminisced about that record-setting day many times, often together, sometimes apart, and even during their enshrinement in the Naismith Memorial Basketball Hall of Fame. Appropriately, they went in together in 1996.

Gervin: "I figured David was going to win, but when I got down to the lobby to go to the game, my teammates and Coach Doug Moe said, 'Ice, we want you to try

Thompson: "It's not too often you have two guys score that many points the same day. That's unbelievable. After I did it I didn't think anybody else could. When George ended up catching me and beating me, I was a little bit upset, but you know there was nothing to be ashamed of coming in second to George Gervin. It was quite an honor."

Gervin: "The next time David and I saw each other, he looked at me like he always did and smiled because he was such a competitor and he had so much respect for me, just like I had for him. It was two individuals who had the ability to put the ball in the basket and that time I won out."

1    One free throw − 8:57 first.

3    Reverse layup − 6:25 first.

6    Baseline jumper and free throw − 5:31 first.

8    Two free throws − 4:37 first.

10    15-foot jumper − 2:49 first.

12    Two free throws − 1:57 first.

14    Layup − 1:12 first.

16    15-foot jumper −:49 first.

18    Layup − :29 first.

20    Top-of-key jumper − :03 first.

22    Left baseline jumper −10:31 second.

25    15-foot jumper and free throw − 10:12 second.

27    Two free throws − 9:48 second.

29    15-foot jumper − 8:35 second.

31    Layup − 7:38 second.

# ICE'S POINT-BY-POINT SCORING RUNDOWN

15-foot jumper − 7:06 second    33

Layup − 6:43 second.    35

Two free throws − 5:26 second.    37

Two free throws − 4:45 second.    39

Left baseline jumper and free throw − 4:16 second.    42

15-foot jumper − 3:43 second.    44

15-foot jumper − 2:54 second.    46

Left baseline jumper − 2:31 second.    48

15-foot jumper − 1:54 second.    50

15-foot jumper − 1:25 second.    52

One free throw − :02 second.    53

Layup − 9:13 third.    55

Two free throws − 7:25 third.    57

Turn-around jumper off left baseline − 5:04 third (SCORING TITLE).    59

Dunk − 9:20 fourth.    61

15-foot jumper −7:15 fourth.    63

**BOB LANIER**

# ABA vs NBA
# NEW vs. OLD
# SCHOOL SCHOOL

The NBA roster offered a constellation of some of the biggest stars in pro sports, including living legend Wilt Chamberlain(third from right), who played in the second inter-league All-Star Game.

The ABA players , however, were not without star power of their own and it manifested itself in a close 106-104 game in 1972, at the Nassau Coliseum in Uniondale, N.Y.

# ABA-NBA All-Star Game Battles

CD2 TRACK 4

**They eyed each other suspiciously, like two rival schoolboys. The popular, established fellow was staring down the new kid on the block. They dressed differently, played the game differently. Heck, they even used different colored basketballs. But they had one trait in common: a desire to be recognized as the best.**

Five years before the finest basketball players in the world would be in one league, stars of the established National Basketball Association and the swashbuckling American Basketball Association met in offseason All-Star Games.

**The first exhibition was held in Houston on May 28, 1971. The NBA roster featured a veritable Who's Who of future Hall of Famers — Milwaukee's Oscar Robertson, Boston's John Havlicek and Detroit's Dave Bing — while the ABA team comprised of lesser-known players such as Dallas' Steve Jones, Indiana's Roger Brown and Miami's Larry Jones.**

The final score, however, did not indicate a disparity in talent; the NBA won the first game 125-120. The leagues then played again the following year and the NBA won by an even closer score, 106-104, at the Nassau Coliseum in Uniondale, N.Y.

**"They were playing to prove that there was another option, that their league could be a viable one," said Hall of Famer Bob Lanier, who was voted MVP of the 1972 game after scoring 15 points in 25 minutes. "As you could tell by that game, it was pretty competitive."**

"They ran their offense and we ran our offense," said Mel Daniels, an ABA All-Star with the Indiana Pacers who participated in both games. "We did what we had to do defensively and they did what they had to do defensively. They were very, very, very competitive, hard-fought games. Both teams took pride in them."

Although the 1971 and 1972 All-Star Games were the only ones played between the two leagues, individual NBA and ABA teams did play 155 exhibition games between 1971 and 1975.

Overall, ABA teams won the exhibition series 79-76. They lost the two All-Star Games by a combined seven points. In the 1977 NBA All-Star Game, the first after four ABA teams joined the NBA, 10 of the 24 players in the game were ex-ABA players. The ABA may have begun as a minor league in 1967, but at the end of its nine-year history, it was evident that the quality of play was at a very high level.

"The term triple-double is something that comes up frequently today and it's a big deal when somebody gets one. Oscar averaged a triple-double for one season and almost three or four others. When you have a player of that caliber, you say to yourself, 'How do I stop him?' He was such a powerful player and had such great control that he could move whoever was guarding him all over the floor. There was nothing Oscar Robertson couldn't do."

JOHN HAVLICEK

# CHAPTER 5
# ONE-MAN SHOWS

## OSCAR ROBERTSON:
### THE ORIGINAL TRIPLE-DOUBLE

### Brilliance is sometimes not quantified until the accomplishment is processed and re-analyzed.

Certainly when Oscar Robertson of the Cincinnati Royals averaged 30.8 points, 11.4 assists and 12.5 rebounds in the 1961-62 season, everyone knew he was great. But the statistic "triple-double" had not yet been conceived. The idea that achieving double figures in the three primary offensive categories was something special had not yet become the focus of basketball experts or fans. The Big O, as Robertson was rightfully called, was, in fact, a full two decades ahead of the term, which is what we often expect of genius.

But as the Magic Johnsons of the world began reaching double figures in three categories in multiple games, the statisticians and the hoop historians had a common response, which was: If you think *that* is special, what about Oscar Robertson? It was a full *season* of consistent brilliance, and a record worthy of comparison to some of the Wilt Chamberlain monuments. It is doubtful anyone will ever score 100 points in a game. It is equally doubtful that anyone will average a triple-double for an entire season.

### Oscar Robertson was one of a kind.

## OTHER CHAPTER 5 MOMENTS

Miller's 8.9-Second Mission
Impossible

The Texas Tornado
Bernard King's Double 50s

Joe Fulks Goes for 63
(Before the 24-Second Clock)

Anchors Aweigh
The Admiral Scores 71

Between Myth and Reality Resides
Legend: Wilt Scores 100

Karl Malone
From Flawed to Flawless

# MILLER'S
## 8.9 SECOND MISSION: IMPOSSIBLE

From every corner of the Garden, you could see the horrified expressions of the disbelieving Knicks fans. Hands were clutching heads, faces were buried into palms, mouths were opened wide in shock.

1995 Eastern Conference Semifinals, Game 1
INDIANA PACERS 107,
NEW YORK KNICKS 105
*May 7, 1995*

## THE INDIANAPOLIS STAR

"Where the Spirit of the Lord is, there is Liberty" II Cor. 3:17

SINGLE COPY 50¢

★★★★

**GAME 1: PACERS 107, KNICKS 105**

# Unbelievable!

In just 8.9 seconds,
Reggie stole the show
and a win from N.Y.

| TIME | NEW YORK KNICKS | SCORE | LEAD | INDIANA PACERS |
|---|---|---|---|---|
| :16.4 | | 105-102 | +3 | Miller 3PT JUMP (Jackson) |
| :14.1 | Mason BAD PASS TO #12 | | | STEAL-Miller |
| :13.3 | | 105-105 | TIE | Miller 3PT JUMP |
| :13.3 | (Starks 1+1) (MISS, MISS) | 105-105 | TIE | Mitchell FOULS (P4, PN) |
| :07.5 | | | | WORKMAN FOR JACKSON |
| :07.5 | Mason FOULS (PS, PN) | 105-107 | -2 | Miller (1+1) (GOOD, GOOD) |

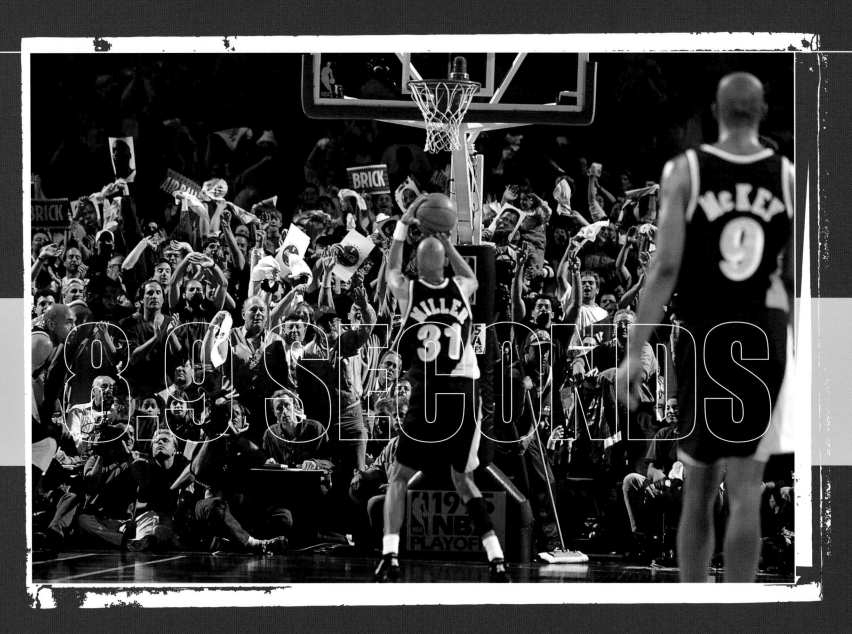

8.9 SECONDS

Nearly 20 years earlier on one miraculous October night, the name elicited a rhythmic chant of love and devotion from all of New York. "REG-GIE! REG-GIE! REG-GIE!" fans screamed for Reggie Jackson, the beloved Yankees slugger. But on the humid spring afternoon of May 7, 1995, the name was derisively spewing out of 19,000 mouths, a serenade of fear and loathing for Indiana Pacers guard Reggie Miller, the quintessential New York villain.

A year earlier, Miller had become New York's ultimate scoundrel when he taunted the Madison Square Garden crowd with throat-grabbing gestures and arrogant insults, but New Yorkers had the last word as the Knicks won a tough seven-game series to advance to the NBA Finals. In Game 1 of the 1995 Eastern Conference Semifinals, it appeared to be more of the same for the Knicks, who led 105-99 with 18.7 seconds left. The Garden crowd was ecstatic, gleefully letting Reggie have it.

The situation was obviously hopeless, but doing what coaches do, Indiana coach Larry Brown instinctively called his final time-out and urged his despondent troops to make a quick basket, give

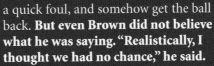

a quick foul, and somehow get the ball back. **But even Brown did not believe what he was saying. "Realistically, I thought we had no chance," he said.**

He was wrong. On the inbound play, point guard Mark Jackson lobbed a pass to Miller right at the three-point line. Reggie whirled and fired in a rainbow jumper over John Starks with 16.4 seconds left. New York 105-102.

New York's Anthony Mason took the ball beneath the Indiana basket, and nervously began patting it in his hands, looking to inbound to a teammate. He had good reason to be fidgety, because the man he was ready to pass the ball to — guard Greg Anthony — was double-teamed by Pacers guards Byron Scott and Miller, and was staggering to the floor after tripping over Miller's left foot. Miller clearly made contact with the Knicks guard, and at that precise moment, Mason decided to pass the ball. But Mason's view was obscured, and Scott never let Anthony fall until Mason had already let the ball go. Immediately, Mason made a gesture to pull the ball back, almost like it was on a tether. But it was too late.

"I saw [Mason] was having trouble finding someone to throw it to," said Miller. "I knew he was going to throw it somewhere. I didn't expect him to throw it to me." Miller caught it, quickly spun around, took one dribble back behind the three-point line, and with Anthony scrambling to get in his face, the skinny Pacers guard confidently rose in the air, and flicked in that odd-looking jumper for a

perfect swish, 105-105 with 13.3 seconds left. From every corner of the Garden, you could see the horrified expressions of the disbelieving Knicks fans. Hands were clutching heads, faces were buried into palms, mouths were opened wide in shock.

**Miller was not yet done.**

On the next possession, John Starks was fouled by Indiana's Sam Mitchell with 13.2 seconds and missed back-to-back free throws. After a Mason rebound and a Patrick Ewing miss, Miller seized the ball.

With 7.5 seconds, Miller was fouled. The rowdy Madison Square Garden crowd strained to raise a disorienting ruckus, but Miller strutted to the line and embraced all of New York's rage. With all the arrogance he could muster, Miller sank both free throws and glared at the screaming fans with a dismissive curl of his lips. As the buzzer sounded and the Pacers ran off the court, **Miller taunted the crowd once again, shouting, "Choke artists! Choke artists!" as the despairing audience hissed his name. To Miller, the ultimate villain, it was a sweet serenade.**

That Sunday afternoon is a permanent part of Pacers' lore. On the floor of Madison Square Garden, where legends from Frank Sinatra to Ringling Bros. and Barnum & Bailey Circus have mesmerized New Yorkers over the years, Reggie Miller was the catalyst the Pacers needed to win the series, and advance to the next round. On that day, he was the greatest one-man show on earth.

## KING B's BACK-TO-BACK 50s

### January 31, 1984 (New York 117, San Antonio 113)

| Min. | FG | FGA | FT | FTA | PTS |
|------|-----|------|-----|------|------|
| 44 | 20 | 30 | 10 | 13 | 50 |

### February 1, 1984 (New York 105, Dallas 98)

| Min. | FG | FGA | FT | FTA | PTS |
|------|-----|------|-----|------|------|
| 41 | 20 | 28 | 10 | 13 | 50 |

**BIG A RESULTS**

SECOND—1ml70yds; cl; Off: 12:55
B3-Surf Club (Vrgr)   14.60   8.20   4.20
E6-Big Izzy (Vnzla)            7.60   4.60
A2-Full Concert (Samyn)               4.40
DAILY DOUBLE (1-3) PAID $47.00
QUINELLA (3-6) PAID $45.30

FOURTH—6 fur; cl; Off: 1:55
B2-Greff (DAgst)   23.80   8.00   4.80
K10-Mcho Dvl (McBth)        3.60   2.60
H7-Dixie's Islnd (Lpz)               3.80
Scratched: Bare Times, French Tab, Young Pretender, Hockey Fan, Space Jet
QUINELLA (2-10) PAID $34.40

Tomorrow's Aqueduct selections: Page 66

# Fantastic 50's

## Amazin' Bernard first in 17 years to score fifty in 2 straight games

By KEVIN KERN

# THE TEXAS TORNADO

First 50-Point Game
[ NEW YORK KNICKS 117, SAN ANTONIO SPURS 113 ]
*January 31, 1984*

Second 50-Point Game
[ NEW YORK KNICKS 105, DALLAS MAVERICKS 98 ]
*February 1, 1984*

## BERNARD KING'S DOUBLE 50S

# BERNARD KING

In the grand pantheon of pro basketball, Bernard King was that rare efficiency expert who mingled among the breathless high-fliers and dazzling improvisation artists.

King's brilliance was in his direct approach to scoring, which he did in bunches. He rarely dabbled in deception with head fakes, behind-the-back dribbles or whirling dervish spins. King's path to the basket was always the same — catch, shoot, score. And so it was on back-to-back nights in Texas during the winter of 1984, when the New York Knicks' cobra-quick small forward registered consecutive 50-point scoring performances. Everything King did against the San Antonio Spurs and Dallas Mavericks was done with his customary efficiency.

**He collected his 100 points during that 48-hour span by shooting 69 percent from the floor (40-of-58) and 77 percent from the free throw line (20-of-26).**

Yet as the game clock wound down to less than 30 seconds in the game against Dallas, Knicks guard Rory Sparrow did not seem to be aware that King was only one basket away from consecutive 50-point games. Sparrow was at the top of the key, dribbling the final seconds off the clock, when he heard a commotion coming from behind him.

"The Knicks bench is screaming, 'Get the ball to King,' they'd like to see him score 50," Knicks play-by-play man Marv Albert said to color commentator Butch Beard.

"They're screaming, 'Give the ball to B!'" said Beard.

"Five on the shot clock …"

The Mavericks' Jay Vincent, however, was playing like he didn't want to be on the wrong end of a record-setting hoop moment. Vincent was clinging tightly to King and denying the pass. Finally, with 12 seconds left on the game clock, King pinned Vincent with his left hand, pushed off and received the pass. In typical King fashion, the historic basket came with his normal, quick-strike, no-nonsense flare. King immediately put the ball onto the floor and drove toward the hole. When Vincent cut off his path, King merely spun in the opposite direction, pulled up and hit a leaning, off-balance jumper that swished cleanly through the nets.

**"Bernard looking for 50,"** Albert pronounced, **"and he's GOT IT! Back-to-back 50s for Bernard King!"**

Later, Sparrow was thankful that his fellow Knicks had screamed at him. "If I didn't give it to him, my teammates would have killed me," Sparrow said. "Heck, I would've killed myself."

# BACK-TO-BACK

# The score was 19-18 . . . and that was after four quarters. During another 48-minute contest, the two teams combined to take 128 free throws, or one every 22.5 seconds.

Each of those instances occurred in the early NBA, at the time known as the Basketball Association of America (BAA), and the founding fathers were obviously very nervous about the future. They had seen the present, and it was flat-out ugly.

So in 1954, a man named Danny Biasone recommended the use of the 24-second shot clock, which increased the pace of the game, and, of course, scoring.

Before teams were forced to shoot in a time frame, however, Joe Fulks of the Philadelphia Warriors scored 63 points in one game. That occurred two seasons before the 19-18 game, making Fulks' feat one of the more staggering accomplishments in the history of professional basketball, regardless of the era.

# Joe Fulks Goes for 63
### (And That Was Before the 24-second Clock)

Philadelphia Warriors 108, Indianapolis Jets 87 • February 10, 1949

*"That night, we didn't even get to eat dinner," said George Senesky, who was Fulks' teammate. "We were coming back from somewhere, and I think we played Indianapolis. The plane had trouble landing, and we flew around for over an hour, and they were unloading the fuel. We all had to get in the back of the plane because they thought the landing gear couldn't come down. So, we just went right from the airport to the arena. We just went right out; we didn't have time to eat dinner or anything."*

Fulks was a one-man maelstrom in a 108-87 victory over the Indianapolis Jets, making 27 of 56 shots and nine of 14 free throws. Along the way he shattered the record for most points in one half (33); field goals; and field goal attempts. The Jets had no answers for the 6-foot-5 Fulks, nicknamed "Jumpin' Joe," who made spinning one-handers, running shots with either hand

and two-handed set shots. The Jets threw five different players at Fulks to no avail. At one point Indianapolis coach Burl Friddle, in mock seriousness, tried to substitute one of his players for Fulks.

Fulks' record stood for 10 years, five of those after the 24-second clock was adopted.

"To me," Senesky said, "that's still a record because that was done before the shot clock."

While Wilt Chamberlain supporters may argue with Senesky since Wilt had 100 points in a game, the magnificence of Fulks' accomplishment is best captured by this fact: In NBA history, only seven men — Chamberlain, David Thompson, Elgin Baylor, David Robinson, Michael Jordan, Pete Maravich and Rick Barry — have scored more points in a single game. And, obviously, each did it after the introduction of the shot clock.

# "To me, that's still a record because that was done before the shot clock."
**GEORGE SENESKY**

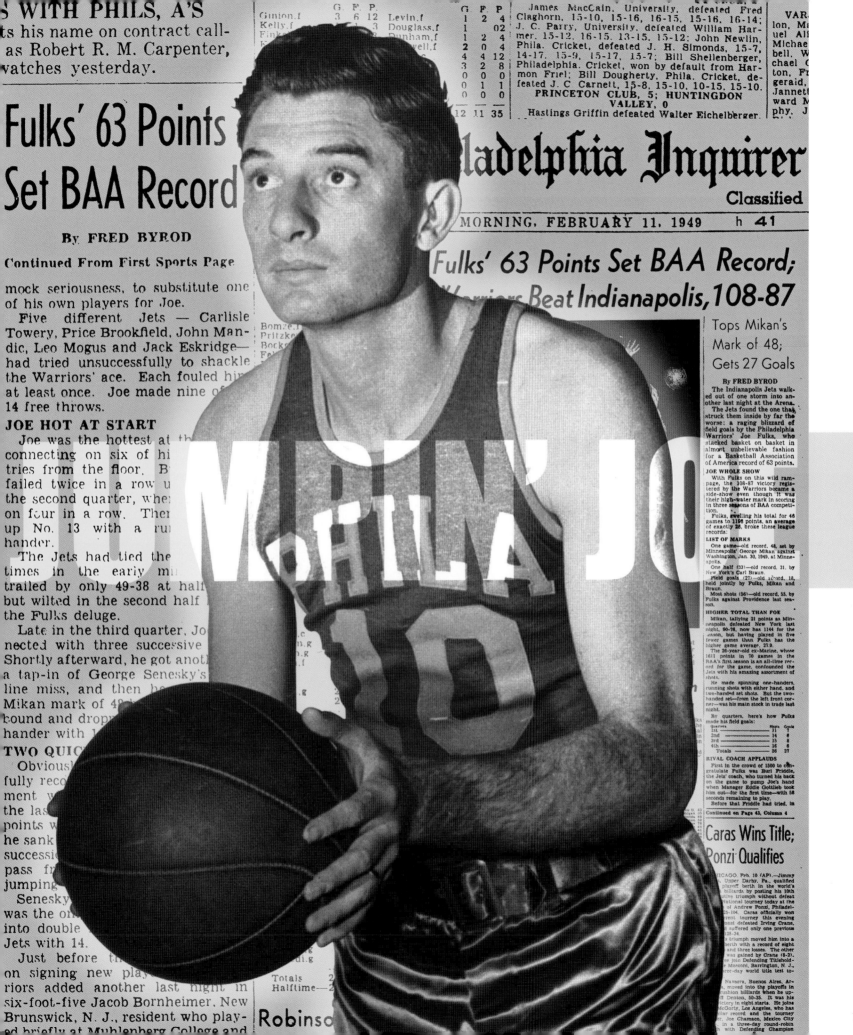

**CD2**
TRACK
**9**

[ SAN ANTONIO SPURS 112, LOS ANGELES CLIPPERS 97 ]
*APRIL 24, 1994*

# ANCHORS AWEIGH:
# THE ADMIRAL SCORES

*When a man stands 7-feet, 1-inch tall, and his body seems to have been sculpted out of a thick slab of granite by the basketball gods, it is not unreasonable to expect him to behave like an intimidating low-post Goliath.*

David Robinson, however, has never fit the mold, much in the same way that a seven-footer does not fit the mold of a Navy officer, or in much the same way that a world-class athlete does not fit the mold of someone who scored a 1320 on his SAT.

Robinson is a master of God, Mother & Country, academics and the saxophone — and, oh yes, the blocked shot, drop step and rim-rattling dunk. He also is a practitioner of basketball's more aesthetic skills.

**On the final day of the 1993-94 regular season, Robinson indisputably proved that, becoming only the fourth man in NBA history to top 70 points in a game when he scored 71 points in a 112-97 victory over the Los Angeles Clippers.** Only Wilt Chamberlain (six times), Elgin Baylor and David Thompson (one each) had ever scored 70 points or more in an NBA game.

In joining that select group, Robinson also edged Orlando's Shaquille O'Neal for the league scoring title by one of the tightest margins in NBA history. Not since the 1977-78 season when George Gervin edged David Thompson by .07 points (27.22 to

27.15) had a race been as close as Robinson's 29.788 average over O'Neal's 29.346. O'Neal complained later that the Spurs ran every play for Robinson, but Gervin, who was on hand to watch Robinson break his franchise mark of 63 points in one game, saw it differently.

"I did what I had to do back then and David did what he had to do," Gervin said. "I told him to take full advantage of the afternoon because he didn't want to look back with any regrets. The guys were behind me when I scored my 63 and the guys were behind David today. That takes you to another level."

Spurs coach John Lucas did run practically every play for Robinson, but he battled double- and triple-teams from the Clippers for much of the game. They even slowed the game down, holding the ball to cut down on Robinson's chances for the title. None of it worked, as he used every move in his shooting arsenal to hit on 26 of 41 field goals and 18 of 25 free throws.

**"That's the hardest I've worked all year," Robinson said. "I looked up at the scoreboard and saw 71 points and said, 'My goodness, 71 points.' I just had to shake my head."**

# BETWEEN MYTH AND
# REALITY RESIDES LEGEND:
# WILT SCORES

[ PHILADELPHIA WARRIORS 169, NEW YORK KNICKS 147 ]

*MARCH 2, 1962*

# Wilt: Pinball Wizard

Wilt Chamberlain was a tired giant when he arrived in Hershey, Pa., on March 2, 1962. Despite playing for the Philadelphia Warriors, Chamberlain lived in New York, where he embraced and enjoyed the lifestyle. On game days, he took the train to Philadelphia. On this day, the game was in Hershey, and he caught a train from New York at 8 a.m.

He had not had the benefit of sleep during the night.

But he still felt strong. He was still Wilt, *The Big Dipper*.

Later, he felt lucky. Or, more accurately, he entered *The Zone*, the divine area all basketball players seek, where an electric feeling envelops your body and suddenly, you feel perfection. Wilt entered *The Zone*, and *The Zone* entered Wilt at an unlikely place — Hershey Park Arena, where he passed time before the game, playing pinball and shooting an air rifle at the penny arcade. "It seemed like whatever I touched, I was breaking record after record," he said. "I just knew I was on. I completely destroyed all existing shooting records there — an omen of things to come."

*The record was demolished with flourish and fury. It was a feat of Herculean proportions and as time has passed, it has taken on mythical qualities. One hundred points. By one man. No one has approached it, not even Chamberlain, the man who achieved it. The next highest one-man scoring performance in NBA history is 78 points, also by Chamberlain. On March 2, 1962 at age 25, Wilt was so overpowering that he could never come close to matching himself.*

Only 4,124 were in Hershey, Pa., to witness the game, which Chamberlain and the Philadelphia Warriors won 169-147 over the New York Knicks. Years later, however, Chamberlain said he figured well over 10,000 people he'd met claimed to be in the stands that night.

**The details of the night are still in dispute. The broadcast of the game was not found for 32 years, and only because a University of Massachusetts student named Jim Trelease was able to pick up a Philadelphia radio station from his dorm room when his radio was positioned properly. He heard on the midnight news that Chamberlain had scored 100 points and part of the game broadcast was going to be replayed. So he taped it, played it several times, stored it with his teenaged possessions and didn't find it again for three decades.**

All the specifics are hazy, mythical and mysterious. Chamberlain said he scored the 100th point on a dunk. Others say it was on a soft lay-in. Everyone at the game claims that fans were so excited that they came out of the stands to mob Chamberlain. Some, including radio announcer Bill Campbell and several players, say the game ended after the last basket

answer: I can't.

"It was like holding up a tree that had been cut and was about to fall down," said Darrall Imhoff, one of the beleaguered Knicks. "You had to keep the thing from collapsing on you. I remember many a time I never took a step, yet I moved into the hoop. My sneakers were smoking."

After the first quarter, Wilt had 23 points. By halftime, it was 41. With a 28-point third quarter, he was up to 69 points. As Chamberlain's totals grew, Warriors public address announcer Dave Zinkoff began telling the crowd how many points Wilt had. "That's 81," Zinkoff would boom. Kids began chanting, "Give it to Wilt! We want 100!"

"I think that's what changed everything," said Warriors teammate Al Attles. "When he started calling, '81 … 83,' I think there was a conscious effort to get the ball to Wilt. Otherwise, we really wouldn't have been cognizant of it."

With 1:30 left, Chamberlain had scored 98 points. He stole an inbounds pass but missed a layup. His next shot was right under the basket. He missed again. The rebound went to teammate Ted Luckenbill, who fed the ball to Wilt. Again, maddeningly, he

**"It was like holding up a tree that had been cut and was about to fall down," said Darrall Imhoff, one of the beleaguered Knicks. "You had to keep the thing from collapsing on you. I remember many a time I never took a step, yet I moved into the hoop. My sneakers were smoking."**

because the fans could not be cleared off the floor. Others say the floor was cleared and it continued. The official box score, which is the permanent record, lists the final score at 169-147, but Campbell said at one point in the broadcast that the score was 169-150. Later, he said it was 169-146.

That, of course, is how legends are made.

**What is not in question is that Chamberlain was supernatural on that night. A career 51 percent free throw shooter, Chamberlain made his first nine and ended the night making 28 of 32. Asked to explain how, Chamberlain said: "I can't."**

That gave him something in common with the Knicks centers, who when asked to stop Chamberlain had the same

missed. Less than 50 seconds were left, and Luckenbill again grabbed the rebound, kicked it back outside to Joe Ruklick, who passed it inside to Chamberlain. The Dipper rose up and softly dropped the ball into the basket. Or did he dunk?

At one time, Chamberlain was sensitive about the record because it was portrayed as the zenith of his career. With so many other records, Chamberlain almost felt his other accomplishments were minimized. But he changed.

**"As time goes by, I feel more and more a part of that 100-point game," he said before passing away on October 12, 1999. "It has become my handle, and I've come to realize just what I did. I'm definitely proud of it."**

# Drivin' With Mr. Wilt

| Q1 | Q2 | Q3 | Q4 | TOTAL |
|----|----|----|----|-------|
| 23 | 18 | 28 | 31 | 100 |

At the end of his epic night, Wilt was justifiably tired. No sleep the previous night. One hundred points. Numerous arcade records demolished. The Big Guy was ready to drop.

One of the lesser known stories is that when he did finally get some rest, members of the vanquished Knicks were on hand. Wilt hitched a ride back to New York, with several Knicks players. The two teams were going to play a game in New York the next night.

"I fell asleep immediately," Chamberlain recalled. "But I kept waking up and I could hear them talking about the game and saying, 'Can you believe what the SOB did to us?' Every time I woke up, they were still talking about what this SOB had done. So when they dropped me off at my door, I said, 'This SOB wants to thank you guys for the ride.'"

Undoubtedly it was a sincere expression of gratitude. First he plays against a defense that he pierces for 100 points, then the same defenders give him a ride home. What more could anyone expect?

### WILT CHAMBERLAIN'S 100-POINT GAME
#### MARCH 2, 1962, AT HERSHEY, PA.

**Philadelphia Warriors (169)**

| | Pos. | FGM | FGA | FTM | FTA | Pts. |
|---|---|---|---|---|---|---|
| Paul Arizin | F | 7 | 18 | 2 | 2 | 16 |
| Tom Meschery | F | 7 | 12 | 2 | 2 | 16 |
| Wilt Chamberlain | C | 36 | 63 | 28 | 32 | 100 |
| Guy Rodgers | G | 1 | 4 | 9 | 12 | 11 |
| Al Attles | G | 8 | 8 | 1 | 1 | 17 |
| York Larese | | 4 | 5 | 1 | 1 | 9 |
| Ed Conlin | | 0 | 4 | 0 | 0 | 0 |
| Joe Ruklick | | 0 | 1 | 0 | 2 | 0 |
| Ted Luckenbill | | 0 | 0 | 0 | 0 | 0 |
| Totals | | 63 | 115 | 43 | 52 | 169 |

**New York Knickerbockers (147)**

| | Pos. | FGM | FGA | FTM | FTA | Pts. |
|---|---|---|---|---|---|---|
| Willie Naulls | F | 9 | 22 | 13 | 15 | 31 |
| Johnny Green | F | 3 | 7 | 0 | 1 | 6 |
| Darrall Imhoff | C | 3 | 7 | 1 | 1 | 7 |
| Richie Guerin | G | 13 | 29 | 13 | 17 | 39 |
| Al Butler | G | 4 | 13 | 0 | 1 | 8 |
| Cleveland Buckner | | 16 | 26 | 1 | 1 | 33 |
| Dave Budd | | 6 | 8 | 1 | 1 | 13 |
| Donnie Butcher | | 3 | 6 | 4 | 6 | 10 |
| Totals | | 57 | 118 | 33 | 41 | 147 |

Wilt exhales after scoring 100 points as fans and teammates Ted Luckenbill and York Larese [right] celebrate the Big Fella's monumental accomplishment.

# KARL MALONE:

## From Flawed to Flawless

**CD2 TRACK 11**

1997 Western Conference Semifinals, Game 4
**UTAH JAZZ 110,
LOS ANGELES LAKERS 95**
*MAY 10, 1997*

# 18 for 18

### Delivering Perfection
### From the Free Throw Line

| MIN. | FG | FGA | REB. |
|------|-----|-----|------|
| 39 | 12 | 27 | 9 |

| ASST. | FT | FTA | PTS. |
|-------|-----|-----|------|
| 3 | 18 | 18 | 42 |

It is the equivalent of a street musician winning a Grammy, or one of the Three Stooges winning an Oscar. Had anyone predicted it after the 1985-86 season, even the record-setter would have laughed, because when **Karl Malone was a rookie, he made only 48.1 percent of his free throw attempts. That easily made him one of the worst free throw shooters in the league.**

In fact, that year, 33 players attempted 400 or more free throws. Of those 33, Malone had by far the worst free throw shooting percentage. The next closest was Houston's Hakeem Olajuwon, who was considerably better with 64.5 percent from the line.

From that beginning, it would have been foolish to predict that Malone would not only one day set the NBA record for most free throws made in a career, but, perhaps more impressively, set the playoff record for most free throws made without a miss.

On May 10, 1997, in a Western Conference semifinals game against the Los Angeles Lakers, Malone was a perfect 18-of-18 from the line. No player has ever attempted as many free throws without missing at least one in a playoff game.

**"That was really a satisfying record," Malone said. "I knew early in my career that I had to get better or I wasn't going to play late in the fourth quarter. Shooting free throws is something that every NBA player should be able to do well. That's why they call them free throws. Because they are free."**

Malone's improvement from the stripe was dramatic. In his second season, he made 59.8 percent of his free throws. The next year, it was 70 percent. And in the 13 seasons since, he has made less than 70 percent only once, and flirted with 80 percent on several occasions. After the 2000-01 NBA season, Malone had made 8,636 free throws, the most in the history of the league.

**"Karl Malone is the hardest-working player I've ever met," said Utah coach Jerry Sloan. "His approach to free throws is like his approach to everything else. He wants to be the best. It says a lot about him that he made himself a great free throw shooter. But if you know Karl Malone, you're not surprised."**

2000 Sydney Olympics

[ USA 106, FRANCE 94 ]

*SEPTEMBER 25, 2000*

"The turning point in the game was when Vince Carter dunked the ball. I think everybody was in awe, and nobody thought he was going to attempt that, but to me that was probably the greatest play in basketball I've ever seen."

JASON KIDD

# CHAPTER 6
# POWER MOMENTS

# SEVEN-FOOT VINSANITY:
## CARTER FLIES OVER FRANCE'S WEIS

## Scientists will tell you that man lacks the ability to fly.

Birds do it, bees do it, but men do not … except in the rare case of Air Canada, Vince Carter. At the 2000 Olympics in Sydney, France's Frederic Weis, all 7-foot-2 of him, was standing in the lane, minding his own business, perhaps prepared to take a charge from Carter, star of the Toronto Raptors, during a preliminary Olympic game.

Carter, however, did not become Vinsanity without reason. As he approached the edge of the lane some 12 feet away from the hoop, Carter took off, cocked the ball back behind his right shoulder, and with a ferocious bit of pure, unadulterated, Superman-like, able-to-leap-tall-players-in-a-single-bound power, leapt right over the Frenchman's head.

The dunk unfolded so fast that it was almost too hard to comprehend. The crowd roared and his teammates chest-thumped him, but no one truly realized the power of the moment until the television replays were shown, proving, quite conclusively that …

## Man can fly.

### OTHER CHAPTER 6 MOMENTS

| | | |
|---|---|---|
| Basketball Evolution | John Starks Invades Rare Air | Chocolate Thunder Erupts |
| Michael Jordan: Dunk Historian | Spud Webb Wins Slam Dunk | Darryl Dawkins' Backboard Breakers |

# BASKETBALL EVOLUTION
## Michael Jordan:
# DUNK
## HISTORIAN

• • • •

Historically, basketball has been no different than technology. Each constantly evolves and it seems that no matter what heights the great players reach, there is always someone right behind them raising the bar even higher. Take the dunk, for example, and listen to one of the masters describe the evolution of one of basketball's most spectacular plays.

"The game of basketball has always been about increasing the norm. When you look at the history of basketball, you see each generation taking something the previous generation did, and improving on it. In the early days of the NBA, there weren't that many players who shot jumpers. As you get into the '50s and '60s, you have guys like Jerry West, Mr. Clutch, and Oscar Robertson, who took the jump shot to a new level.

  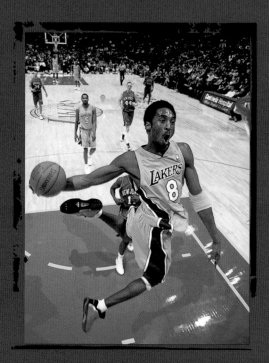

"The same is true with the slam dunk. As the athletes got better, the slam dunk became more of an art, especially in the ABA, where they had the first slam dunk contest. You can see on that film the creativity of the ABA players, who brought a lot of that into the NBA when the two leagues joined. And that improved the level of play in the NBA.

"I think everyone knows I've always been competitive, and even though

one of my early heroes was **David Thompson,** who they called **Skywalker,** I obviously admired **Julius Erving, Dr. J,** and based a lot of my game on trying to compete with what he had done. I followed Thompson when he was in college because I was growing up in North Carolina, and he was playing at North Carolina State, but it was Dr. J who took the dunk to the next level. I tried to take it one step further, and I think today's players, like **Vince Carter** and **Kobe Bryant,** are trying to take it to even another level.

"If you look at the slam dunk contest at the ABA All-Star Game in 1976, Dr. J was the first to take off from the foul line. I did it the first time in 1985 on All-Star Saturday in Indianapolis. And Vince Carter did it in 2000 in Oakland.

"But each time, there was a difference and it represented progress.

"When Dr. J took off, he *ran* up the court, jumped from the foul line, and dunked.

"When I did it, I *dribbled* up the court, took off from the foul line, and dunked. That is harder to do because you've got to get your rhythm together, make sure you pick up the dribble at the right time, still keep an eye on the foul line, and take off. No one really noticed it at the time, that I dribbled, but that was my way of improving on what Dr. J did. That's taking it to the next level.

"And then at All-Star Weekend in 2000, Vince Carter took off, ran up the court, jumped from the foul line, and dunked with two hands. That's even harder to do. That was his way of improving on what I had done. That is the evolution of how change happens.

"Improving the game is all about increasing the norm. That's what we did in the slam dunk contest. Dr. J ran, I dribbled and Vince Carter used two hands.

# That is the evolution of the dunk."

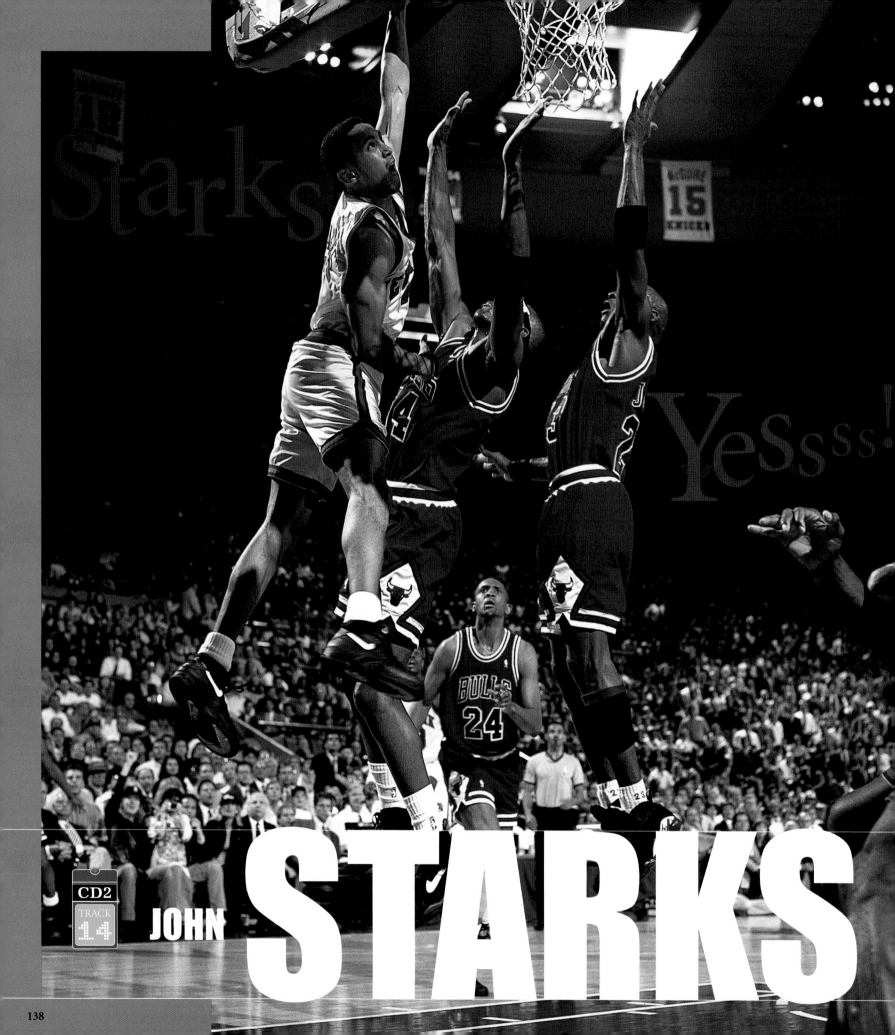

JOHN STARKS

*As hard as it is to sometimes imagine, Michael Jordan did not own the exclusive hang-gliding rights to the airspace during all those memorable playoff wars with the New York Knicks in the 1990s.*

John Starks, the mercurial guard for the Knicks, pulled off a levitating act worthy of any Air Jordan highlight video with an explosive baseline slam over Jordan and Horace Grant in the final minute. The spectacular basket helped preserve a 96-91 victory in Game 2 of the 1993 Eastern Conference Finals, although, ultimately, it still made no difference in the result of the series. When Jordan was in Chicago, the Bulls always won; the Knicks always lost.

The war, that is. But on this night, not the battle. The Knicks had blown a 14-point third quarter lead in Madison Square Garden as the Bulls stormed back to within 91-88 with 1:26 remaining. But as the clock ticked down under a minute, Starks had the ball up to the right of the foul line, and created his moment of glory. Knicks center Patrick Ewing stepped up and set a pick on Chicago guard B.J.

Armstrong, allowing Starks to cut hard to the baseline, leaving Armstrong completely out of defensive position. As Starks reached the baseline, he curled to his left, and cut straight down the baseline, where

Grant popped up to cut off his path. But just as Starks' feet touched the paint, he exploded upward, switching the ball from his right to left hand.

The 6-foot-10-inch Grant leaped up with the 6-foot-5-inch guard, leaning backward with both hands extended, and Starks leaned his body into Grant's chest, fully extending his left arm with the ball high above his head. But suddenly, there was company in the airspace above the rim. Jordan had come roaring down the lane at the last second to take a swipe at the high-flying Starks. But Starks kept elevating, and with a sudden ferocity, threw down a vicious dunk.

"Starks ... YESSSS!!!," bellowed Marv Albert on the NBC national telecast.

"What a move by Starks!!! He was able to sky to the basket!"

"It felt good," said Starks. "It felt as good as something can feel in this world."

**On that night, he was in another world usually populated only by Jordan. Rare Air, indeed.**

INVADES RARE AIR

# SPUD WEBB
# WINS
# SLAM

1986 All-Star Slam Dunk Contest
*FEBRUARY 8, 1986*

As the contestants in the 1986 All-Star Slam Dunk contest gathered on the floor of Dallas' Reunion Arena, Anthony "Spud" Webb appeared to be a low-lying ground cover amidst a forest of redwoods. At 5-foot-7, Webb could have passed for a ball boy. As he stood beneath the rim lining up for one of his dunks, the sellout crowd of 16,573 seemed to adore him. He was their vicarious thrill ride. "He's America," said Mike Fratello, his coach with the Atlanta Hawks. **"Tomorrow, every father and son will be out in the driveway trying to dunk. If Spud can do it, anyone can. People will be talking about him on their way to work or riding the bus."**

What they had to talk about on this All-Star Weekend was the sight of this mighty mite soaring to the most unlikely slam dunk championship in the history of the celebrated event.

It hardly mattered what sort of dunk he performed, though they were all routinely magnificent. The crowd loved everything he did. **He lobbed a pass to himself, caught it and slammed it through the basket. He did twisting 360-degree, double-pump, two-handed slams and 180-degree, two-handed, backward dunks. He bounced one ball off the backboard, soared a foot above the rim, caught it in midair and jammed it down for a perfect score.**

And with each dunk, the adoring crowd chant-

# DUNK

ed, screamed and hollered. Here was Spud Webb, a native of Dallas, with hands so small they could not palm a ball, meaning he had to jump even higher, but he was every bit as good as players a foot taller, such as his spectacular Atlanta teammate, 6-foot-8 Dominique Wilkins. The fans wanted victory for their diminutive Everyman, and that's exactly what they got.

**"Spud was the people's choice,"** said Dave Cowens, one of the five judges who were clearly **influenced by the crowd. "We tried to be as fair as we could, but I don't know how he could have lost it."**

# Chocolate
# THUNDER
# ERUPTS

## DARRYL DAWKINS BRINGS DOWN THE HOUSE — TWICE

## Imagine for a moment comedian Chris Rock in Shaquille O'Neal's body.

Introducing Darryl Dawkins, the slam-dunking, backboard shattering, outrageous comedian/center for the Julius Erving-era Philadelphia 76ers. Dawkins gained attention when he went directly from high school to the NBA, but his celebrity was solidified in less than a one-month span of the 1979-80 season. The 6-foot-11, 252-pound Dawkins created a national sensation when he shattered two fiberglass backboards during games, and subsequently proclaimed himself "CHOCOLATE THUNDER."

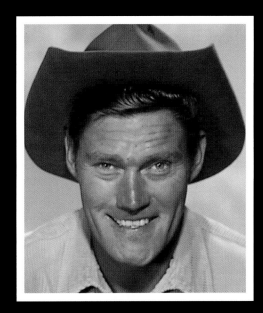

## CHUCK CONNORS
### SHOOTS DOWN A BACKBOARD

The first dunk came on November 13 in Municipal Auditorium against the Kansas City Kings. Dawkins slammed the ball down over Kings forward Bill Robinzine and brought down both the rim and the entire backboard. Glass scattered everywhere, and the game was delayed for more than an hour while the shattered backboard was replaced. While Dawkins may not have gone to college, he was an accomplished elocutionist, a master of rhyme and a soulful descendent of Muhammad Ali. Thus the dunk became: **Chocolate Thunder Flyin', Robinzine Cryin', Teeth Shakin', Glass Breakin', Rump Roastin', Bun Toastin', Wham, Bam, Glass Breaker I am Jam.**

Twenty-three days later, in the Philadelphia Spectrum, before a smallish crowd of 9,286, Sixers guard Doug Collins was driving in from the left baseline, drawing coverage from San Antonio center Dave Corzine. When Corzine arrived, Collins dished it to the hard-charging

Dawkins, who despite his size could sky with the greatest leapers. Dawkins exploded to the basket and coiled the ball with two hands behind his head, nearly touching his shoulder blades. Then with all the power he could generate from his gigantic body, Dawkins slammed the ball down at the rim like a human wrecking ball.

**This time, all the glass did not explode onto the floor. Dawkins simply ripped the rim to the floor. But the backboard glass was a mess, with spider-webbed cracks all over.**

"I didn't mean to destroy it," said the 22-year-old Dawkins. "It was the power, the Chocolate Thunder. I could feel it surging through my body, fighting to get out. I had no control over it."

**"I started to rush in to help out," said San Antonio's George Gervin. "Then I saw Double D cock the ball behind his head. I got the hell out of there. I knew what was coming. I had seen his Kansas City act on the TV replay. In slow motion. It was scary."**

Long before dunks had names, before seven-footers weighed 280 pounds and could run with the wind and jump to the ceiling, backboards were not safe from NBA players. Chuck Connors — yes, the same Chuck Connors who starred as Lucas McCain on "The Rifleman" television series from 1958-1963 — was, in fact, the first player in league history to break a backboard, although it was not a feat of Herculean strength.

On November 5, 1946, 4,329 fans showed up at the Boston Arena to watch the Celtics play the Chicago Stags in the first game of the first season. Connors, Boston's 6-7 center, was warming up when he took a set shot that began as harmless, and ended with glass all over the floor because the rim had not been properly secured to the backboard.

"During the warmups, I took a harmless 15- to 20-foot set shot, and CRASH, the glass backboard shattered," Connors recalled years later.

Celtics publicist Howie McHugh finally tracked down another backboard at the Boston Garden, where Gene Autry's rodeo was performing. Problematic for McHugh was that the backboard was located in the bull's pen. So he bribed a couple of cowpokes to retrieve the backboard and a truck transported it to the Arena.

When the game ended, the Stags had won 57-55. It was an inauspicious start for Coach John "Honey" Russell's Celtics, who would end up going 22-38 that season and tie for last place in the Eastern Division.

"Russell never forgave me for breaking the backboard," Connors recalled. "He thought I'd ruined his season before it started."

A moment is sometimes great because it is unique or unforgettable. Boston's Tony Lavelli was an accordion player who doubled as a basketball player, and produced one of many great, unusual moments in NBA history.

144

# CHAPTER 7
# UNUSUAL MOMENTS

# LAVELLI SERENADES

**Negotiations with No. 1 draft picks can sometimes be hostile affairs with each side arguing about provisions, incentives or wording. That is life in the NBA, and it has been that way since the beginning, although in the early days, the dickering was usually over thousands rather than millions of dollars.**

Money, however, did not apply to the contract negotiations of Tony Lavelli, whose key demand was unique in sports history. Lavelli didn't ask for suites on the road, limos, private jets or his own hair stylist. He merely wanted to play basketball — *and* be the halftime entertainment.

Lavelli was the Boston Celtics' No. 1 pick in 1949 after a distinguished career at Yale, where he earned All-America honors. His true love, however, was music. An accomplished accordion player, Lavelli refused to sign unless he was allowed to play his instrument at games. The Celtics conceded and Lavelli was guaranteed a minimum of 25 halftime performances at the rate of $125 a performance.

**While his teammates were discussing strategy at halftime, Lavelli was serenading fans with ballads such as "Lady of Spain," "Granada," and selections from "William Tell."**

In basketball lingo, when a shooter gets it going and the ball is continuously ripping through the net, that shooting streak is often described as "sweet music." Only in Tony Lavelli's case could such a description apply literally.

## OTHER CHAPTER 7 MOMENTS

The Dream Team
A Global Phenomenon

The Yugoslavian Phonetic Obstacle
Course: Starring Johnny Most

NBA Fashion
Not Always Fantastic

The Age of Aquarius
It's The Hair!

Mop-Up Time
Tablecloths Save Pacers-Spurs Game

Déjà Vu All Over Again
Spurs Fans Washed Out

Return of the Cagers
Not Too Jazzy

Crouching Tiger, Hidden Mavericks
Dick Motta's Roaring Halftime

The photo with Puerto Rico was typical of what the Dream Team experienced during its 1992 march to Olympic gold.

# THE
# DREAM TEAM
## A GLOBAL PHENOMENON

**CD2 TRACK 18**

By the time they had all gathered for that first, historic team picture, the basketball world had already begun its substantial, meteoric change. It was the summer of 1992, and the greatest basketball team ever assembled – accurately described as *"The Dream Team"* – was preparing to send the popularity of professional basketball onto a dizzying trajectory of total globalization.

But as they gathered in Portland, Ore., for the Olympic qualifying tournament known as the Tournament of the Americas, how could they know the mania that was ahead? How could they anticipate the passion they would generate, especially among the competition?

They were basketball's equivalent of Elvis, the Beatles or Ali. Magic and Bird. Jordan and Pippen. Stockton and Malone. Barkley, Ewing, Robinson, Drexler and Mullin, with one lucky player chosen from the college ranks — Duke's Christian Laettner. They were

the first superstars of a plugged-in generation, beamed to the world 24 hours a day through cable and satellite, the Internet and the never-ending chatter of talk radio.

They traveled from California to Oregon to the French Riviera, and ultimately to Barcelona, and found themselves viewed not as competitors, but as objects of affection and adoration. Their opponents came to measure themselves against the greatest team ever assembled. But ultimately they came to pay homage to basketball deities.

At a party the night before the opening game of the qualifying tournament in Portland, Mexican players lined up in single file to get their picture taken with Charles Barkley. The next afternoon, moments before the U.S. dismantled the Cuban national team by 79 points, the Cubans asked to take a group photo with the entire Dream Team. The ones who were fortunate enough to be close to Michael Jordan squeezed next to him like giddy schoolchildren.

### ★ 1992 USA RESULTS (8-0) ★

| USA | 116 | ANGOLA | 48 |
|-----|-----|--------|-----|
| USA | 103 | CROATIA | 70 |
| USA | 111 | GERMANY | 68 |
| USA | 127 | BRAZIL | 83 |
| USA | 122 | SPAIN | 81 |
| USA | 115 | PUERTO RICO (QUARTERFINALS) | 77 |
| USA | 127 | LITHUANIA (SEMIFINALS) | 76 |
| USA | 117 | CROATIA (GOLD MEDAL GAME) | 85 |

**"As we say in Cuba, 'You can't cover the sun with your finger.'"**

*Cuban Olympic basketball coach Miguels Calderon Gomez, explaining the difficulty of competing against the Dream Team*

# They were basketball's equivalent of Elvis, the Beatles or Ali.

## "Our aim was to lose by less than 45 points."

**VICTOR CUNHA,** Angolan coach

148

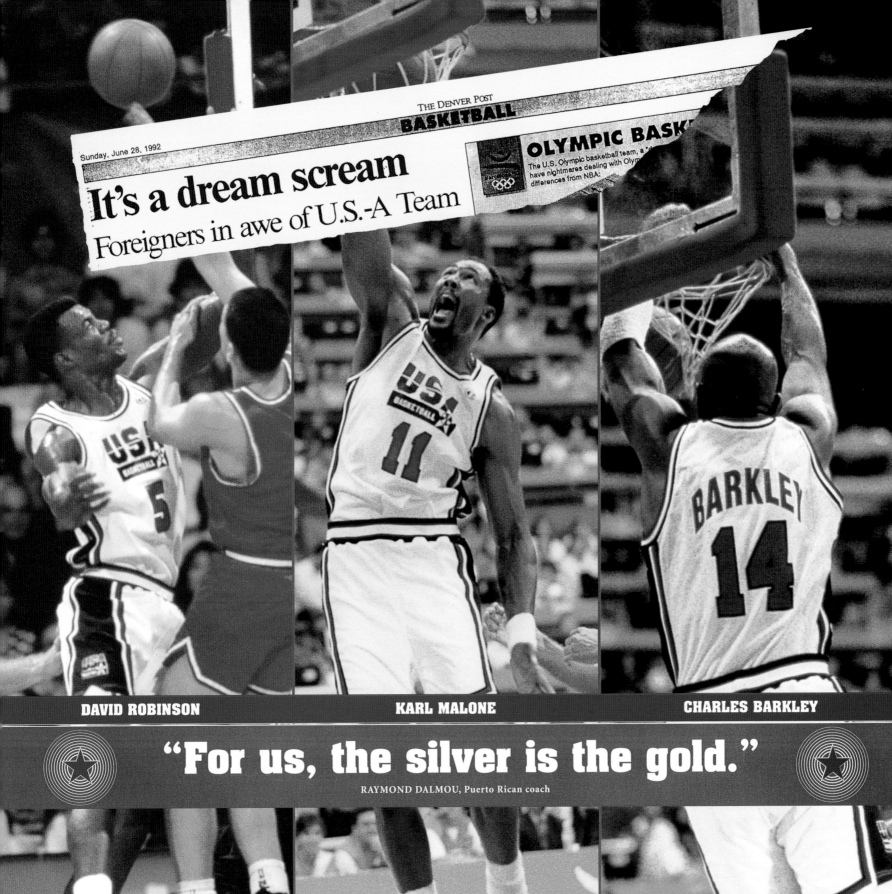

THE DENVER POST

**BASKETBALL**

Sunday, June 28, 1992

## It's a dream scream
### Foreigners in awe of U.S.-A Team

**OLYMPIC BASK**

The U.S. Olympic basketball team, a
have nightmares dealing with Olym
differences from NBA:

**DAVID ROBINSON**

**KARL MALONE**

**CHARLES BARKLEY**

# "For us, the silver is the gold."
RAYMOND DALMOU, Puerto Rican coach

149

> **"I am happy because I played against the best players in the world. I told my mother, 'I took a picture with Magic Johnson after the game.'"**
>
> NELSON TIMOTEO ALVES SARDINHA, Angolan center

"That was a little weird," Jordan said after the 136-57 victory.

It would get even weirder. In the middle of a game, Argentina's Marco Milanesio found himself posting up Magic. Luckily for Milanesio, it was the side nearest to the Argentinian bench — because when he frantically signaled to a teammate seated on the bench, the teammate pulled out a camera and took a historic photo of Milanesio, who now had evidence he could show to his grandchildren that he was indeed on the floor against one of history's greatest players.

It never stopped. During games in Portland, the Dream Teamers were asked for shoes, jerseys, socks, wrist bands — anything to commemorate the moment.

In Barcelona during the opening ceremonies, the photo opportunities continued. Samoans in sarongs, high-fiving Chinese, giddy Frenchmen, not to mention American athletes of every size, shape, and sport, came dashing over to the Dream Team.

After the Dream Team destroyed Angola 116-48 in the opening round, Angolan coach Victor Cunha said, "Our aim was to lose by less than 45 points."

Opponents didn't seem to care that the outcome of the games had been preordained or that the words "gold medal winner" had been scrolled on the side of Mount Olympus eons ago. A 50-point loss would engender only smiles among the defeated. **"For us, the silver is the gold,"** reasoned Puerto Rican coach Raymond Dalmou.

But perhaps the Angolan center Nelson Timoteo Alves Sardinha explained the mood of most of the Dream Team's opponents. "I am happy because I played against the best players in the world," Sardinha said. "I told my mother, 'I took a picture with Magic Johnson after the game.'"

# SIR CHARLES

Charles Barkley never has been at a loss for outrageous words, but the Dream Team experience produced verbal highlights that qualify for the Barkley Hall of Fame. When the Dream Team trained in Monte Carlo, Barkley was incredulous at some of the local customs.

**Barkley on Monte Carlo prices:** "This place is a trip. The people here are very neat, very friendly and very well dressed, but you can't stay here for long. Things cost too much. If you're an alcoholic, this is a good place to come because a beer can cost you $40. You can't afford to be a drunk here."

**Barkley on the proper etiquette involving dinner with Prince Rainier at the Royal Palace:** "We're supposed to stop eating when he stops? But what if we're still hungry? He may have had a snack before he came over."

**Barkley on women sunbathing topless at the beaches and hotel pool:** "I'm quitting this team for the Olympic swim team. I'm going to the pool as long as there are babes with no tops. You'll think I'm Mark Spitz before this week is over."

# THE YUGOSLAVIAN
## PHONETIC OBSTACLE COURSE: STARRING JOHNNY MOST

Johnny Most never apologized for his devotion to the Celtics, and it was his unabashed fanaticism that made him beloved to generations of Boston fans. The Celtics won 11 titles behind Bill Russell, two more with John Havlicek and Dave Cowens, and three more with Larry Bird serving as the franchise players. Anyone who followed those champions on the radio listened to Johnny Most, who was very clear in his approach that the Celtics were the good guys and the opponents were not simply bad guys, but very much closer to jerks.

Most screamed to legions of fans that "**Havlicek stole the ball!**" and that Ralph Sampson was a "gutless big guy who picks on the little people" after he got into a fight with Boston guard Jerry Sichting. In Most's world, Jim Loscutoff became "Jungle Jim" and Washington's Rick Mahorn and Jeff Ruland metamorphosed into "McFilthy and McNasty."

"People think of Johnny and the first thing that comes to mind is a Celtics fanatic," said legendary Knicks announcer Marty Glickman, who gave Most his first broadcasting job in 1948. "But what they should always remember is that he was a great broadcaster. Johnny was as good a basketball announcer as I've ever heard."

**CD2 TRACK 19**

But all sports superstars suffer through slumps. And Most's occurred during the 1988 McDonald's Championship in Madrid, when the Celtics played the Yugoslavian National Team and all those hard-to-pronounce names. As it turns out, Most did not think to prepare before the game, and the tongue-twisters did indeed do some twisting.

"On the right, quickly it goes to … uh … I'm going to have a little trouble with the names at first."

"Now the rebound is picked up by one of the big guys. This one is … uh … Divatch (Divac) underneath. He lost the ball but he gets it back outside to one of the little guards. And the shot is no good. The rebound by … uh …"

"Now quickly to a big guy and now to a lefty. And he lost the ball. And now the little feller. Oh boy, I'm having trouble with the names."

Written words, in this case, do not do the moment justice. The tape was played on a portable recorder when the Celtics flew back to the U.S., and the players, along with everyone else, were roaring.

Most was a little sheepish, but still consistent. After all, the Celtics were the good guys.

> "People think of Johnny and the first thing that comes to mind is a Celtics fanatic, but what they should always remember is that he was a great broadcaster. Johnny was as good a basketball announcer as I've ever heard."
>
> **MARTY GLICKMAN**
> FORMER KNICKS ANNOUNCER

## BLAZING BABBLES

In a profession overrun with sweet warblers and smooth talkers, the late Johnny Most had the caustic voice of a barroom brawl. Radio broadcasters are supposed to be syrupy, elegant poets who craft vivid oral images. Not Most, who sounded like a handful of gravel rumbling around in a small tin box.

From 1953-90, Most delivered his decidedly biased, often hilarious, and always brutally colorful descriptions of the fate of every moment in Celtics history. "He was an institution," said Red Auerbach, Boston's Hall of Fame former coach and general manager. "He was up there by himself, smoking cigarettes, drinking coffee, and every time we got fouled, we were killed."

In a game against the Milwaukee Bucks in 1986, the chain-smoking Most was characteristically careless with the burning ashes, and some floated into his lap. His slacks caught fire, but Most was oblivious to the combustion that quickly grew into smoke and flames. This is what it sounded like on the air that night:

Most: "OOOOOOHHH MY!!!!"

Color analyst Glenn Ordway: "This is a first (laughter) . . . Johnny has (more laughter) . . . lit (even more laughter) . . . his pants are on fire!!!! (uncontrollable laughter)"

As Most recalled the night, he said, "Glenn was getting hysterical. He was laughing so hard, I was laughing hard, I was on fire, and sparks were flying all over the place. We finally got it out, I had a hole, I swear, as big as a baseball."

And a moment unequaled in sports broadcasting history.

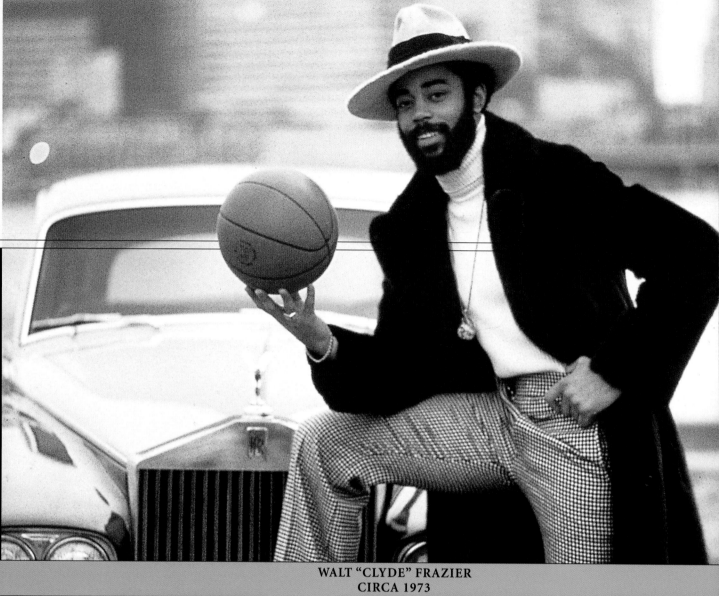

GEORGE GERVIN
CIRCA 1977

WALT "CLYDE" FRAZIER
CIRCA 1973

# SARTORIAL SPLENDOR:
# NBA FASHION:
## NOT ALWAYS FANTASTIC

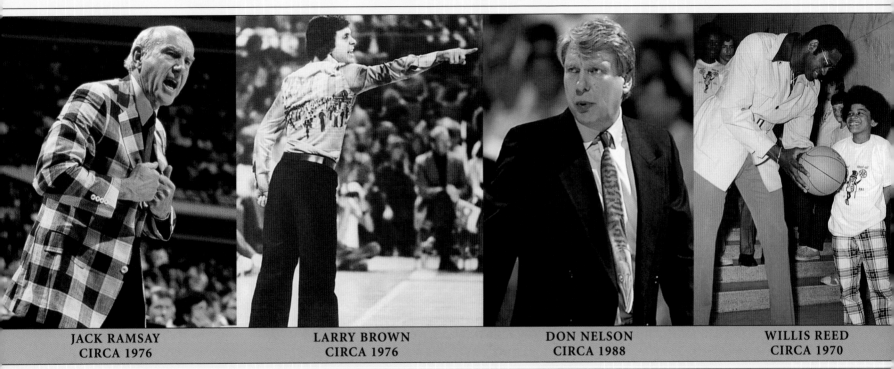

**JACK RAMSAY
CIRCA 1976**

**LARRY BROWN
CIRCA 1976**

**DON NELSON
CIRCA 1988**

**WILLIS REED
CIRCA 1970**

## Once the runway for men in monochromatic suits and black lace-up shoes, basketball sidelines underwent a sartorial revolution beginning in the '70s.

**Y**ears before Larry Brown donned conservative pinstriped suits to patrol NBA sidelines, he was known as the "Modfather." As coach of the ABA's Carolina Cougars and Denver Nuggets, Brown wore overalls at press conferences and bell-bottomed slacks at games.

Jack Ramsay piloted the Portland Trail Blazers to the 1977 NBA title blazing his own fashion statement: plaid with no regard for style. Don Nelson of the Milwaukee Bucks roamed the sidelines wearing his beloved fish tie.

On the court, players made their own statements, acces-sorizing with color-coordinated headbands and wristbands. And don't forget the socks. They were long. Very long.

**"We had a different kind of style back in the ABA,"
remembered George Gervin. "I wore long socks, I think
Julius might have had long socks on, Artis Gilmore wore long
socks, and we kind of had our own identity early on
in our professional careers."**

Over time, the shorts have gotten longer and the headbands more creative. But recently, the socks have been again creeping up toward the knees.

Could bell-bottoms and leisure suits be very far away?

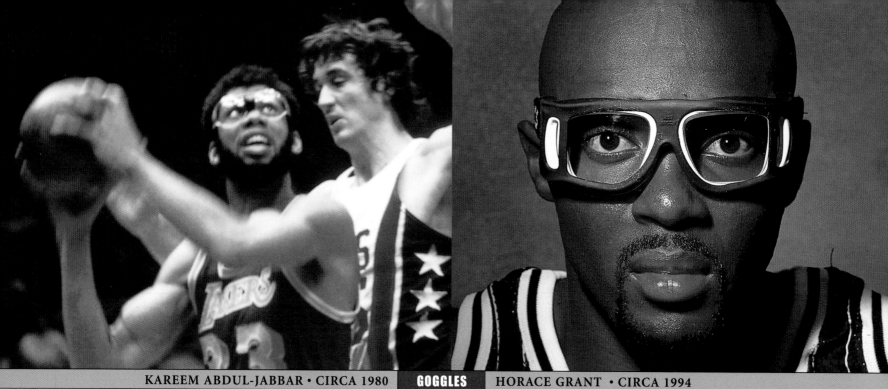

KAREEM ABDUL-JABBAR • CIRCA 1980    **GOGGLES**    HORACE GRANT • CIRCA 1994

ED BADGER (LEFT) AND DICK MOTTA • CIRCA 1974    **SUITS**    PAT RILEY • CIRCA 2000

WILT CHAMBERLAIN • CIRCA 1972 **HEADBANDS** BARON DAVIS • 2001

Some '70s fashions have had a longer shelf life than most thought or hoped they would. While headbands have reappeared on basketball courts throughout the league, short-shorts — quite luckily — are nowhere in sight.

VINNIE JOHNSON • CIRCA 1990 **SHORTS** ALLEN IVERSON AND STEPHON MARBURY • 2001

The Age of Aquarius

# IT'S THE HAIR

IT'S THE HAIR IT'S THE HAIR IT'S THE HAIR IT'S THE HAIR IT'S THE HAIR IT'S THE HAIR IT'S

CD2
TRACK
21

"Julius Erving had a big afro that flew in the air when he was flying in the air. And Artis Gilmore had a big afro. **BUT DARNELL HILLMAN HAD THE 'FRO OF 'FROS.** We had a different kind of style back in the ABA."

GEORGE GERVIN

★ DARNELL HILLMAN CIRCA 1976

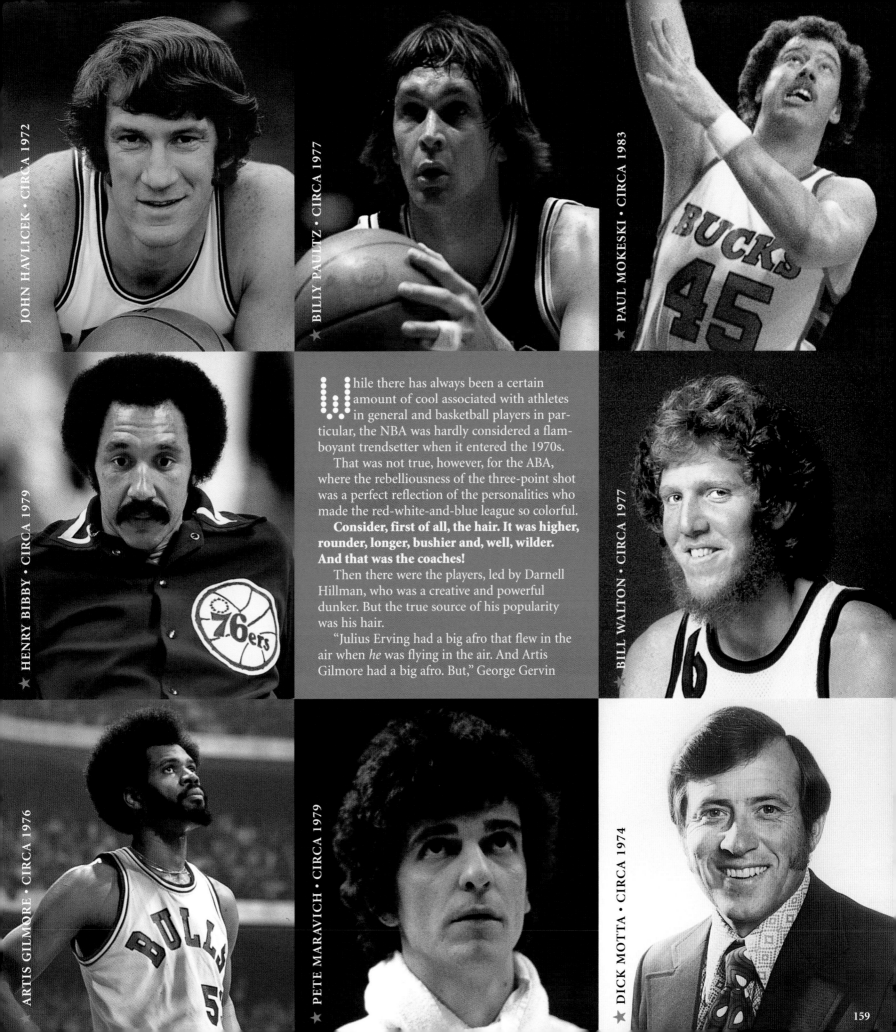

JOHN HAVLICEK · CIRCA 1972

BILLY PAULTZ · CIRCA 1977

PAUL MOKESKI · CIRCA 1983

HENRY BIBBY · CIRCA 1979

BILL WALTON · CIRCA 1977

ARTIS GILMORE · CIRCA 1976

PETE MARAVICH · CIRCA 1979

DICK MOTTA · CIRCA 1974

While there has always been a certain amount of cool associated with athletes in general and basketball players in particular, the NBA was hardly considered a flamboyant trendsetter when it entered the 1970s.

That was not true, however, for the ABA, where the rebelliousness of the three-point shot was a perfect reflection of the personalities who made the red-white-and-blue league so colorful. **Consider, first of all, the hair. It was higher, rounder, longer, bushier and, well, wilder. And that was the coaches!**

Then there were the players, led by Darnell Hillman, who was a creative and powerful dunker. But the true source of his popularity was his hair.

"Julius Erving had a big afro that flew in the air when *he* was flying in the air. And Artis Gilmore had a big afro. But," George Gervin

159

RODMAN

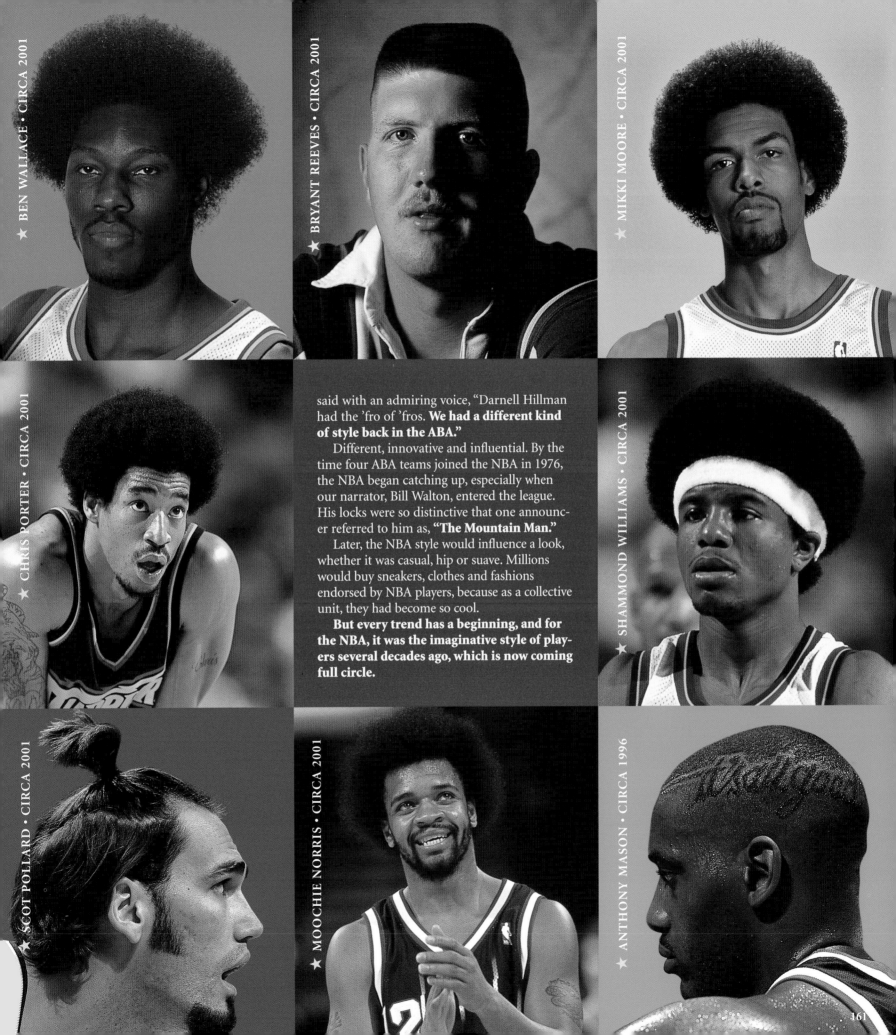

★ BEN WALLACE • CIRCA 2001

★ BRYANT REEVES • CIRCA 2001

★ MIKKI MOORE • CIRCA 2001

★ CHRIS PORTER • CIRCA 2001

★ SHAMMOND WILLIAMS • CIRCA 2001

said with an admiring voice, "Darnell Hillman had the 'fro of 'fros. **We had a different kind of style back in the ABA."**

Different, innovative and influential. By the time four ABA teams joined the NBA in 1976, the NBA began catching up, especially when our narrator, Bill Walton, entered the league. His locks were so distinctive that one announcer referred to him as, **"The Mountain Man."**

Later, the NBA style would influence a look, whether it was casual, hip or suave. Millions would buy sneakers, clothes and fashions endorsed by NBA players, because as a collective unit, they had become so cool.

**But every trend has a beginning, and for the NBA, it was the imaginative style of players several decades ago, which is now coming full circle.**

★ SCOT POLLARD • CIRCA 2001

★ MOOCHIE NORRIS • CIRCA 2001

★ ANTHONY MASON • CIRCA 1996

BY WAYNE WITT

*The ABA lasted for nine years, and the final regular season game on April 7, 1976, in San Antonio was one of the most memorable. But not because of the game itself. I was working for the Spurs at the time as their public relations director, and we were playing the Indiana Pacers. It was not only the last game of the season, but the playoffs also started the next night, so we had to finish the game, no matter what.*

# MOP-UP TIME

## TABLECLOTHS SAVE PACERS-SPURS GAME

[ SAN ANTONIO SPURS 96, INDIANA PACERS 75 ]

*APRIL 7, 1976*

We got into the second quarter and this huge thunderstorm — in West Texas we call it a **trash floater** or a **frog strangler** — erupted. Our roof was in such bad shape that water began streaming steadily down into the arena. It not only fell on the fans, it also leaked onto the playing floor. We couldn't reschedule because of the next night's playoffs, but we didn't want to refund money for tickets. So the decision was made to play. But, first, we had to do something about the water that was right at midcourt next to the scorer's table. There was no way we could ignore it.

A catering company was close by, so we ran over and borrowed some big, white tablecloths. After we mopped up the floor as well as we could, we put the cloths on the court and taped them so they wouldn't move. The coaches and referees then met and agreed to modify the rules, which became: No pressure defense outside the three-point line and no fast breaks.

We won the game 96-75, but that was secondary to the spectacle. **I still remember people sitting in the stands with open umbrellas so they wouldn't get soaked.** It is supposed to be bad luck when you have an open umbrella indoors, but we won the game, so for us on that night, the rain, the tablecloths and the open umbrellas seemed to be pretty good luck.

And we set a record. Ninety-six points in the rain? Find another team that has done that.

# San Antonio Express-News

Serving San Antonio and South Texas since 1865

TODAY'S
WEATHER

High 76°
Low 56°
Partly cloudy
Details, Page 12C

This page is recyclable

4A Saturday, November 5, 1994 F

## Dome's deluge taken in stride

# Spurs soaked in opening-day loss

While it is tempting to say that there must be something in the water in San Antonio, as far as the Spurs and their home court are concerned, there is something that the water is in — whether it is the action at HemisFair Arena or the stands at the Alamodome. Almost two decades after the Spurs and Indiana Pacers had to play a game with tablecloths covering the court, a high-pressure water cannon erupted in the Alamodome and spurted out more than 2,500 gallons of liquid confusion per minute.

This time, against such force, umbrellas were useless. This was not about a few drops, or even a steady downpour. This was an indoor tidal wave that left spectators running for cover and the Spurs-Golden State Warriors game delayed for 50 minutes. It was later

# Déjà Vu All Over Again
## Spurs Fans Washed Out

discovered that an uncapped smoke detector, apparently set off by a pregame fireworks display, had been the culprit behind the deluge.

For those who happened to be in the line of fire, spirits may have been dampened some-what, although most took the inconvenience in stride. The Spurs did what they could to make their drenched patrons more comfortable, including bringing in towels from nearby hotels and replacing beer that had given a new definition to "watered-down."

It all occurred on November 4, 1994, which was opening night. So, after waiting all summer to see their Spurs play, the spectators present had to stay patient a bit longer. And though the team eventually took the floor, the result was a washout for San Antonio fans — their Spurs slipped up, 123-118.

# "We played in Loyola Fieldhouse, which was basically off the floor about four feet ...

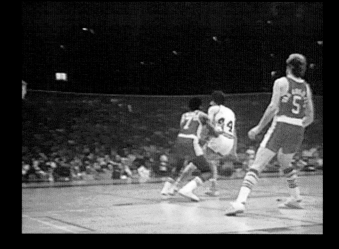

## Return of the
# CAGERS:
## Not too Jazzy

BY DAVE FREDMAN

# ... so they put a big net around the entire court so people wouldn't fall off."

**PETE MARAVICH**

The last 27 years of working for the Jazz has included many unforgettable experiences, but I would have to say that one of the most unusual occurred in the first year when the team was in New Orleans.

I was one of the team's original employees, working as an intern in public relations and ticket sales in the first year. **Our home-court was supposed to be the Superdome, but it wasn't quite ready in 1974, so we had to scramble around for places to play.** The primary homes were Municipal Auditorium, which sat about 8,000 and Loyola Fieldhouse, which sat about 6,600.

**Loyola Fieldhouse was an old gymnasium where the basketball floor was raised about four feet above the seats.** It was almost like a stage. When the Players Association found out about it and the league inspected it, they decided it wasn't safe for the players because they could run off and fall into the stands trying to save a ball. So, it was decided that they would put a net around the court for the players' safety. **So, that year, the games at Loyola Fieldhouse were played with a safety net around the entire court.**

There was a lot of talk about the old days when basketball first started and everyone played with cages around the court. It was definitely different. When teams would come in for the first time, they would look at the nets and say: "This place ought to be in the Hall of Fame."

**The nets were mainly for safety, but as it turned out, they weren't needed. I don't recall any time when a player ran into them, so it ended up being more of a spectacle.** You had to get used to watching the game through a net from the stands, and that made it very interesting. Eventually, we got used to playing there. When the weather got warmer, visiting teams had a hard time because there was no air-conditioning. The nets also really confused them, so we had a real home-court advantage. After losing about 45 of our first 50 games, we won about half of our remaining games.

We ended up kind of liking the nets.

167

CD2
TRACK
25

CROUCH

## DICK MOTTA'S ROARING HALFTIME

One of the toughest jobs in pro basketball has to be coaching an expansion team. When Dick Motta became coach of the expansion Dallas Mavericks in 1980, he said that the team consisted of three types of players – those with bad contracts, bad attitudes or those players who were just plain bad.

"And some of them were two out of three," Motta said.

While Motta could understand the difficulty of competing with more talented teams, he refused to accept a lack of effort. So early in the first season, he employed one of the most unusual motivational tactics in the history of the NBA.

"We were in Oakland to play Golden State," said Motta, who is now

retired and the owner of a bed and breakfast inn in Bear Mountain, Idaho. "The circus was in town and at halftime of a game where we weren't rebounding very well, we were walking to the locker room and I saw a tiger, a monkey and this young woman who had them both on a leash. I see them bring out a six-foot basket and they give the monkey these basketballs. So I said, 'I gotta see this thing. I can *always* talk to the players.' Well, the monkey is shooting baskets, and he's not missing anything and the tiger's running and grabbing the rebounds with his mouth. His mouth is large enough to hold a basketball. Before they did their act, the girl is walking by with the tiger on a leash. I asked her, 'Is that a nice tiger?'

"'Yes, it *is* a nice tiger,' she said. So I asked her, 'Would you do me a favor? Could you bring that tiger into the dressing room after your act?'"

So with the tiger stationed outside the locker room, Motta lit into his players.

"If you don't start rebounding, I'm gonna do something about it," he screamed. Then he went to the door, and came marching in with the leashed tiger. "If you don't start rebounding, this tiger is going to eat every one of you."

"Our reaction was, we started to scatter," said Jim Spanarkel, who was one of the frightened Mavericks players. Spanarkel said, however, that they moved extremely slowly, "because here was this tiger with a head the size of a computer screen," and *no one* wanted to startle him."

To this day, none of his players are sure if Motta was joking. "I think they believed me," said the coach. "They did not think it was very funny. And I probably should have gotten the monkey in uniform, come to think of it. Heck, he shot a lot better than any of the guards I had that year."

HIDDEN MAVERICKS

NG TIGER

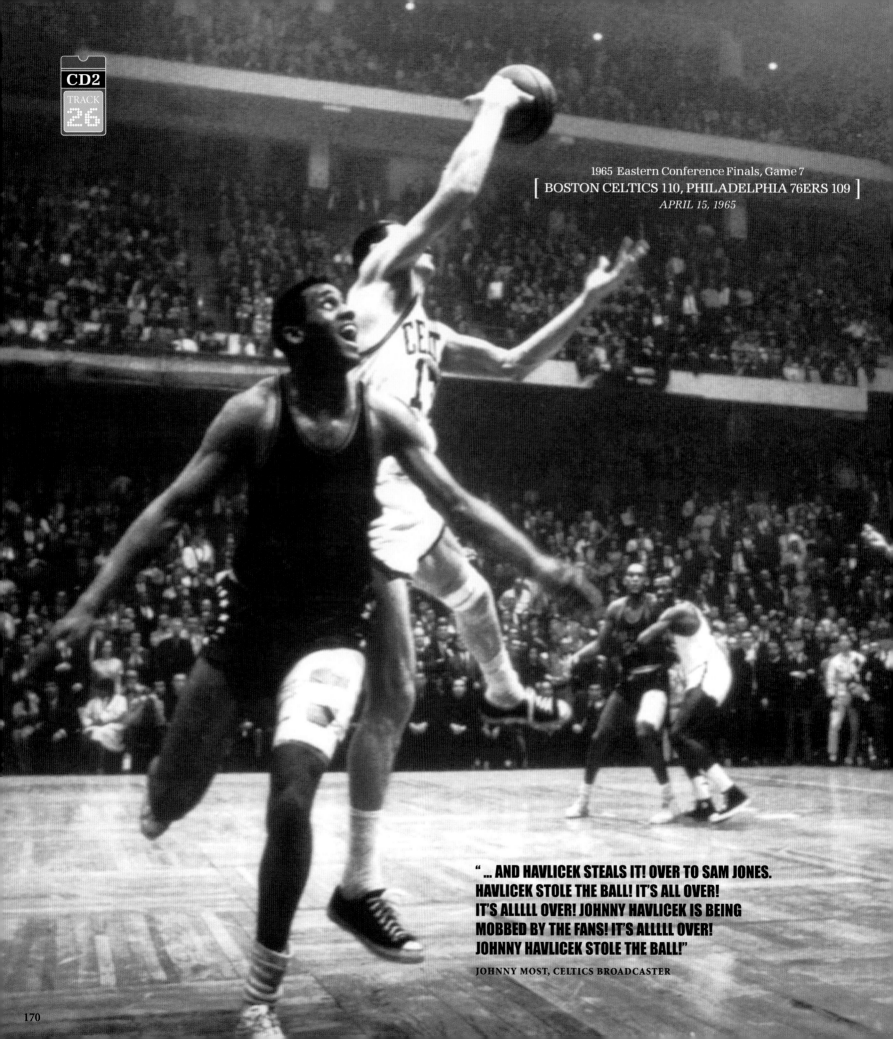

1965  Eastern Conference Finals, Game 7

[ BOSTON CELTICS 110, PHILADELPHIA 76ERS 109 ]

*APRIL 15, 1965*

" ... AND HAVLICEK STEALS IT! OVER TO SAM JONES.
HAVLICEK STOLE THE BALL! IT'S ALL OVER!
IT'S ALLLLL OVER! JOHNNY HAVLICEK IS BEING
MOBBED BY THE FANS! IT'S ALLLLL OVER!
JOHNNY HAVLICEK STOLE THE BALL!"

JOHNNY MOST, CELTICS BROADCASTER

# CHAPTER 8
# MONUMENTAL MOMENTS

**The scene:** *Bill Russell, the consummate big-game player, is beside himself after an unimaginable error. With five seconds left in regulation of Game 7 of the 1965 Eastern Division Finals, Russell's inbound pass strikes the overhead guy wire that supports the Boston Garden basket, and fierce rival Philadelphia gets possession. The Celtics are ahead 110-109, but Philadelphia will have the last shot. After a timeout, the referee hands Philadelphia's Hal Greer the ball …*

# HOW I STOLE THE BALL

## By John Havlicek

Before Hal Greer inbounded the ball, I was looking for an edge and knew that when the official hands the ball to the player, he has five seconds to get it into play.

So I started to count to myself: one thousand one, one thousand two, one thousand three, one thousand four

and I had my eye on Chet Walker, who I was guarding, and the ball. When I got to one thousand four, I realized Greer was having a problem getting the ball in. I took a little peek and I was able to see him release it. The pass was sort of a lob and if I had my back turned I never would have been able to see it.

But by taking that little extra peek, I knew that I could get my hand on the ball

and control it and deflect it to Sam Jones. I did. And the rest is history.

## OTHER CHAPTER 8 MOMENTS

"That was a driven team, with a lot to prove to a lot of people. What's amazing about our streak, looking back, is that there were no last-second shots, no heroics like that for us. There were games when we didn't play well, but we always found a way to win. Once the streak started rolling, it was the snowball effect. You could see that teams didn't think they could beat us. It was like Mike Tyson when he was beating everybody. It was just a matter of which punch was going to knock you out."

JIM McMILLIAN, Lakers starting small forward

Wilt Chamberlain (13) scoops a shot for an easy two points as Clyde Frazier and the Knicks helplessly look on.

# THE STREAK

## THE LAKERS' INCREDIBLE 33 GAMES

Jerry West (44) makes his move thanks to Wilt Chamberlain's bone-crushing pick on the Knicks' Clyde Frazier.

After more than two months of absolute perfection, the Los Angeles Lakers found their mortality on a Sunday afternoon in Milwaukee, where the Bucks ended the most remarkable winning streak in NBA history. For 33 games – from November 5, 1971, until January 9, 1972, – the Lakers could do no wrong on the basketball court.

First-year coach Bill Sharman had blended together aging future Hall of Famers Wilt Chamberlain and Jerry West with rising young stars Gail Goodrich and Jim McMillian, and the result was a superb basketball machine.

The streak began with a victory over defending Eastern Conference champion Baltimore, and rolled on through a 134-90 destruction of Atlanta on January 7. Then, two days later on a nationally televised Sunday afternoon game against Kareem Abdul-Jabbar and the defending NBA champion Milwaukee Bucks, the Lakers saw their two-month string of perfection come to a shocking end with a 120-104 loss.

**"We lost it, Milwaukee didn't win it,"** said McMillian afterward. This attitude permeated the Los Angeles locker room, and with good cause. The Lakers played a sloppy, uninspired game, committing 24 turnovers and shooting 39 percent from the floor.

Yet the most obvious reason why the Lakers streak ended was because of the graceful, unstoppable presence of the young Milwaukee center, Abdul-Jabbar, who three years later would be traded to the Lakers and become the centerpiece of the franchise for 14 years. **In only his**

**third season in the NBA, the graceful 7-foot-2 giant had already become the league's most lethal offensive force.** Against the Lakers, Kareem scored 39 points, grabbed 20 rebounds, and capped off the afternoon with a stinging punch to the jaw of Lakers forward Happy Hairston, that sent Hairston sprawling to the floor.

Early in the second quarter, Abdul-Jabbar became angered when fouled by Hairston and took a hard swing at him. The punch landed solidly and left Hairston out cold for several seconds. Oddly enough, it was Hairston's teammate Chamberlain – perhaps relating all too well to the physical abuse that Kareem endured every night – who calmly led the Bucks' center away from the action.

**"I simply lost my temper," said Abdul-Jabbar,** who was not ejected from the game, only receiving a personal foul.

**"Sure I fouled him," said Hairston. "Fouls are a part of basketball, but slugging isn't."**

During the course of the winning streak, Sharman had written a speech he intended to deliver to the players when the streak ended. But after the game, Sharman never made the speech. "Oh,

I had a couple of corny things written, but I didn't read them today," he said. "I don't want to take away anything from Milwaukee, but this is one of the weakest games we've played in a long time. However, in the long run, I think this defeat will help us. We made some mistakes when we were winning, but it's hard to learn from them when you've won a game."

As he left the visitor's locker room, McMillian looked back at a group of reporters and asked the most pertinent question of the evening: **"What's our record?"**

**The answer was 39-4. "That's still not too bad,"** said McMillian, sporting a sly grin as he flipped the collar of his overcoat up and headed into the chilly Milwaukee night.

Not bad at all. A few months later, the Lakers had added a few more records that would eventually be broken, but not for a long while. After that season, the Lakers held records for most victories in a season (69), most games scoring 100 points (81), and most victories on the road (31). But best of all, by the end of the year, the Lakers were also NBA champions, a fitting conclusion to such a prosperous and record-setting season.

Jerry West (44) and the Lakers couldn't muscle past Oscar Roberston and the Bucks to keep the streak alive.

Gail Goodrich has the inside track on Kareem Abdul-Jabbar for a loose ball.

Kareem Abdul-Jabbar (33) played a large role in ending L.A.'s winning streak but Wilt Chamberlain and the Lakers regrouped to post a then NBA regular-season record of 69 wins.

## THE LAKERS' 33-GAME WINNING STREAK

**VS**

| Nov. 5 | @ Baltimore | 110-106 |
|---|---|---|
| Nov. 6 | @ Golden State | 105-89 |
| Nov. 7 | New York | 103-96 |
| Nov. 9 | @ Chicago | 122-109 |
| Nov. 10 | @ Philadelphia | 143-103 |
| Nov. 12 | Seattle | 115-97 |
| Nov. 13 | @ Portland | 130-108 |
| Nov. 14 | Boston | 128-115 |
| Nov. 16 | Cleveland | 108-90 |
| Nov. 19 | Houston | 106-99 |
| Nov. 21 | Milwaukee | 112-105 |
| Nov. 25 | @ Seattle | 139-115 |
| Nov. 26 | Detroit | 132-113 |
| Nov. 28 | Seattle | 138-121 |
| Dec. 1 | @ Boston | 124-111 |
| Dec. 3 | @ Philadelphia | 131-116 |
| Dec. 5 | Portland | 123-107 |
| Dec. 8 | @ Houston | 125-120 |
| Dec. 9 | @ Golden State | 124-111 |
| Dec. 10 | Phoenix | 126-117 |
| Dec. 12 | Atlanta | 105-95 |
| Dec. 14 | @ Portland | 129-114 |
| Dec. 17 | Golden State | 129-99 |
| Dec. 18 | @ Phoenix | 132-106 |
| Dec. 19 | Philadelphia | 154-132 |
| Dec. 21 | @ Buffalo | 117-103 |
| Dec. 22 | @ Baltimore | 127-120 |
| Dec. 26 | Houston | 137-115 |
| Dec. 28 | Buffalo | 105-87 |
| Dec. 30 | @ Seattle | 122-106 |
| Jan. 2 | Boston | 122-113 |
| Jan. 5 | @ Cleveland | 113-103 |
| Jan. 7 | @ Atlanta | 134-90 |

38,387

# KAREEM OF THE CROP:

## ABDUL-JABBAR SETS SCORING RECORD

**LOS ANGELES LAKERS 129, UTAH JAZZ 115**  *APRIL 5, 1984*

With his brooding sensibilities and his ethereal airs, Kareem Abdul-Jabbar always carried himself with the ultra-hip demeanor of a cutting-edge jazz messenger. There was a cool, detached genius to his every move on the court, a fluid style that separated him from all the other 7-foot behemoths who roamed the paint.

And if jazz was an original American art form, then so too was Abdul-Jabbar's jazzy athletic creation, the elegant sky hook.

During a 20-year NBA career that spanned three decades, Kareem became the all-time leading scorer in the regular season (38,387 points), playoffs (5,762) and All-Star Game (251). On April 5, 1984, when he surpassed Wilt Chamberlain for the regular-season scoring record, it was only fitting that the shot he used to break the mark was his trademark sky hook.

Midway through the fourth quarter of a 129-115 victory over the Utah Jazz, Abdul-Jabbar caught Magic Johnson's pass in the low post, with 7-foot-4-inch Utah center Mark Eaton pushing him from behind. Eaton planted his sizeable body right into the small of Kareem's back.

This was how it always was for Abdul-Jabbar. Because there were so few big men who matched Abdul-Jabbar's on-court finesse and intelligence, there was only one weapon his opponents could use to blunt his singular basketball artistry: grinding, brute force.

So the slam dance began. Eaton, the league's top shotblocker (4.28 blocks per game), pushed and shoved, Kareem retaliated with his usual stylish touch. He faked to his right toward the paint, and Eaton bit, leaning far enough in the wrong direction to render himself useless. Kareem quickly wheeled in the opposite direction, toward the left baseline. By the time Eaton tried to recover, it was too late.

Kareem uncoiled his entire 7-foot-2-inch frame like a lithe dancer, pirouetting on the ball of his left foot, stretching his left arm up as a protective shield into Eaton's chest, sweeping his right arm up far over his head like a slow-motion catapult. As his hand finished its sweeping motion at the top of its arch, Kareem's fingers gently flicked the ball on a sweet rotating path to the basket some 10 feet away, just beyond the reach of the straining Eaton.

As the ball swished through the nets, Abdul-Jabbar elevated his career point total to 31,420, one point more than Chamberlain's previous NBA record. And there were still almost 7,000 points to be scored over the next five seasons, most of them with the most beautiful shot in NBA history.

# STOCKTON

**CD2**
**TRACK 29**

## Stockton's milestone assists Nuggets loss

**By Mike Monroe**
Denver Post Sports Writer

SALT LAKE CITY — The Denver Nuggets last night were witness to basketball history at Delta Center, and they did little else but watch, in seeming wonder, as one of the game's greatest players reached a significant milestone.

Utah Jazz guard John Stockton became the NBA's all-time leader in assists with 6:22 left in the second quarter of the Jazz's 129-88 thrashing of the Nuggets, who appeared belpless as Stockton and mates and a sellout crowd reveled in the occasion.

The loss was the Nuggets' worst of a season that has gone horribly awry.

### ASSISTS LEADERS

The NBA's top 10 career assists leaders:

| | | |
|---|---|---|
| 1. John Stockton | 9,921 | 9,927 |
| 2. Magic Johnson | 9,887 | |
| 3. Oscar Robertson | 9,061 | |
| 4. Isiah Thomas | 7,392 | |
| 5. Maurice Cheeks | 7,211 | |
| 6. Lenny Wilkens | 6,955 | |
| 7. Bob Cousy | 6,917 | |
| 8. Guy Rodgers | 6,476 | |
| 9. Nate Archibald | 6,454 | |
| 10. John Lucas | | |

the Nuggets by a bigger margin than the 41 by which they were thumped last night.

The Nuggets and Jazz are exhibits in total contrast. Utah has won 1 games in a row. Denver has lost eight of its last nine, and been blown out o three of its last six. None, though, has been as embarrassing as last night's.

"It's disrespectful to each team staff, disrespectful to ourselves," Nuggets forward Brian Williams said of Denver's pitiful performance. "I just don't know what it is."

The fact the Nuggets provided only

Only six times in the 27 years the franchise has existed, in both the ABA and the NBA, has anyone beaten

Please

## 9,921 ASSISTS

# -TO- MALONE:
## A RECORD-SETTING MATCH
### The Utah duo established scoring and assist milestones together

*It is not mandatory to be a basketball graybeard to understand the subtle hoop artistry of John Stockton and Karl Malone, but it surely helps. Old-school eyes are wise enough to look past all the exhilarating athleticism of today's hip-hop rim rockers, and instead appreciate the below-the-rim squareness of Stockton-to-Malone.*

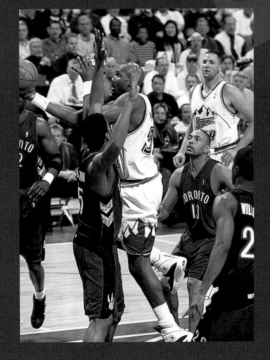

Stockton-to-Malone is not about all the flash and glamour of hang-gliding slams or other such ostentatious trappings of today's game. Instead, Stockton-to-Malone is about how these three words have come to define the mastery of one of basketball's most basic works of art:

**Pick and roll.**

**Stockton-to-Malone is about how two men have become inextricably linked into one forever-hyphenated phrase. You can not have one without the other.** Malone does not shoot without Stockton passing. Stockton does not dish unless Malone receives. So here they are, once again on the same page; inseparable, even in their own individual record-setting achievements.

On December 5, 2000, when Malone passed Wilt Chamberlain to move into the No. 2 spot on the league's all-time career scoring list, how could anyone other than Stockton be the one who tossed him a perfect bounce pass? Five years earlier, when Stockton passed Magic Johnson to become the NBA's all-time career assists leader, there was no one else who could have received the pass but Malone.

It was the middle of the second quarter of a 129-88 blowout over the Denver Nuggets, when Stockton was approaching Magic's league record of 9,921 assists. However, Malone was on the bench, taking his normal second-quarter breather.

**"When he started getting closer and closer [to the record], everybody on the bench started looking at me, saying, 'Check yourself in,'" Malone recalled. "I told them, 'I'm not the coach.'"**

Fortunately, the coach, Jerry Sloan, had a sense of history. When Stockton tied the record, he hurried Malone into the game, and just to make sure things would be done correctly, called a timeout to set up the proper play.

There was really no need for such extra preparation, because there was really no other way for this to go but Stockton-to-Malone. **So with the Jazz leading 47-25, Malone posted up on the left side of the paint, caught a simple bounce pass from Stockton, then stepped back to the baseline and hit a jumper over Denver's Brian Williams.**

# It was so simple. Nothing flashy, nothing jaw-dropping, nothing that made the crowd oooh or aaaah. It was vintage Stockton-to-Malone. A simple pass, a simple shot.

**And five years later when Malone passed the legendary Chamberlain to move into second place on the scoring list behind Kareem Abdul-Jabbar, it was much the same thing. With Utah leading Toronto 40-25 in the second quarter of an eventual 98-84 Jazz victory, Stockton took the ball up court and drifted left, then saw Malone posting up Corliss Williamson.**

Several times earlier, the crowd of 19,288 in the Delta Center had incorrectly anticipated the record-breaking moment and camera flashes popped all over the building like a sparkling light show. But this time, when the lights went off, it was to record history. Malone took another simple pass from Stockton, turned to face up to the hoop, drove past Williamson into the lane and made a scooping finger roll that hit the rim, then the backboard, then went through the hoop. Malone had sur-

passed Chamberlain's total of 31,419 points.

Now there they both are, ahead of all the flashy names like Jordan and Erving, Chamberlain and West, Robertson and Magic. So let the young eyes yawn at Stockton-to-Malone as humdrum, repetitive taskmasters. But the sharper eyes of the basketball cognoscente know better. The old-school eyes hear those three words, Stockton-to-Malone, and see art that is nothing less than a masterpiece.

# Here Comes WILLIS

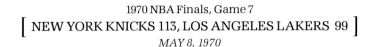

## Reed Spurs Knicks to Title

*When the NBA attempts to capture the essence of its greatness in one, brief, neat 30-second television spot, Willis Reed is lumbering through the tunnel at Madison Square Garden. There are other monumental exploits, including those listed elsewhere in this chapter, but none symbolize the heart, soul and competitiveness of what the NBA player has been all about since 1946 more than Reed at that one moment.*

The date was May 8, 1970. The atmosphere within Madison Square Garden was thick with tension. Game 7 of the NBA Finals, matching the New York Knicks and the Los Angeles Lakers, would begin momentarily. Four nights before, in Game 5, Reed, the Knicks' captain, had crumbled to the floor, tearing a muscle in his right thigh. The Knicks held on to win that night, but lost Game 6 when Reed could not play.

**Pregame warmups had already begun, but Reed was nowhere to be seen. All eyes were fixed on the tunnel leading to the Knicks' dressing room. Slowly, a white-clad figure appeared in the darkness, limping into the bright lights of the Garden. The next several seconds provided perhaps the most dramatic moment in NBA history.**

"When Willis came out onto the court," said former Knick Bill Bradley, "it was like the place exploded. Chills were going up

and down everyone's spines."

**Knicks forward Dave DeBusschere quickly looked at the Lakers, and they were almost in a trance. The facial expressions of Jerry West, Elgin Baylor and Wilt Chamberlain were revealing. "At that point," DeBusschere said, "I thought we were winners. I thought they were defeated."**

Reed scored only four points that night, but the impact of his powerful entrance gave New York a perceptible edge, and the Knicks, who got 36 points and 19 assists from Walt Frazier, went on to claim their first championship with a 113-99 victory.

"I didn't want to be sitting on my porch someday with my grandchildren, saying to myself, 'If I had only tried to play that night,'" Reed said. "Every time I see somebody, they say, 'I was there, I was there.' We figured right now it's up to about 300,000 people."

> ## "I didn't want to be sitting on my porch someday with my grandchildren, saying to myself, 'If I had only tried to play that night.'"
> **WILLIS REED**

**Dave Stallworth [9] leads the Knicks bench in celebration.**

**Reed eludes Wilt for an open look.**

**Broadcaster Howard Cosell can't escape Bradley and DeBusschere's championship exuberance.**

# CLYDE GLIDES
## TO GAME 7 HEROICS

**A**lthough Willis Reed was the inspiration for the Knicks' dramatic Game 7 victory in the 1970 NBA Finals, Walt Frazier was the catalyst. Reed's stirring entrance into the arena gave the Knicks an emotional lift, but he scored only two baskets and left the game. It was Frazier's 36 points, 19 assists, seven rebounds and smothering defense that lifted the Knicks to victory. Here are Frazier's reflections:

"My biggest decision before Game 7 of the 1970 Finals was, 'What I am going to wear tonight?' I didn't have that enthusiasm because I didn't know whether Willis was going to play. Only when I got to the Garden did I find out it was dubious whether he would. In the locker room everybody is asking, 'Is Willis playing? Is Willis playing?' Coach Holzman became concerned. He said, 'Hey guys, I don't care if Willis plays or not. We've gotta play, so forget about Reed. Just try to get focused on the game.' So when we left the locker room we still had no idea if Willis would play. People think it was premeditated, that it was planned and we were just waiting until he came out, but we were just as flabbergasted as the crowd and the Lakers.

"I saw the whole Lakers team standing around and staring at this man. And Willis set the tempo. He made the first two shots and that was it. We said, 'The captain is ready. Half of Willis Reed is better than anybody else we could put out there.' So he provided the inspiration, and in a way I provided the devastation. That was perhaps my best game as a player considering what was on the line — a championship. But entering that game I never thought that I had to score, I had to rebound. I just let it happen, I let the game come to me. Normally Holzman was telling me to hit the open man. But in this particular game I was the open man."

# CHICAGO BULLS: THE GREATEST
# "Anybody Else Win 72 Games?"

"THE BOTTOM LINE IS, WHILE I'M STILL ON THE COURT, DON'T TRY TO MOVE ANYONE INTO MY SPOT. I'M THE ONLY ONE WHO WILL DECIDE THAT. ONLY ME."

MICHAEL JORDAN

## 1995-96

| CENTRAL DIVISION | W | L | PCT. |
|---|---|---|---|
| Chicago Bulls | 72 | 10 | .878 |
| Indiana | 52 | 30 | .634 |
| Cleveland | 47 | 35 | .573 |
| Atlanta | 46 | 36 | .561 |
| Detroit | 46 | 36 | .561 |
| Charlotte | 41 | 41 | .500 |
| Milwaukee | 25 | 57 | .305 |
| Toronto | 21 | 61 | .256 |

*Whenever the discussion became heated, as subjects involving sports and politics are wont to do, Michael Jordan had a succinct answer to the question before the panel:*

# Which of the NBA's great championship teams ranked as the best team of all time?

*Jordan's brow would crease, a mock quizzical look would spread across his face, and he would ask rhetorically: "Anybody else win 72 games?"*

**I**t is an impossible task to compare teams from different eras. How can it be determined if Russell's Celtics were better than Bird's, or Magic's Lakers were better than Wilt's?

Yet it is undeniable that for one spectacular season, Michael Jordan's Bulls reached an amazing level of proficiency that no team can claim to match. The Bulls' 1995-96 season — 72 victories and only 10 defeats in the regular season — bettered the previous league mark of 69-13 by the 1971-72 Los Angeles Lakers, who were led by Wilt Chamberlain and Jerry West. Then the Bulls ran through the playoffs with a 15-3 postseason mark on the way to the fourth of six NBA titles in the '90s.

Chicago was a fascinating blend of personalities and talents. There was the cross-dressing, rock-idol rebounding machine Dennis Rodman, and Scottie Pippen, the multitalented forward who was named one of the 50 Greatest Players in NBA History; there was the Zen master head coach Phil Jackson, and a collection of role-players like Ron Harper, Toni Kukoc, Steve Kerr, Randy Brown, Luc Longley and Jud Buechler.

The man who fueled this passionate drive

for perfection, however, was Jordan. The extraordinarily competitive Jordan had a cause that season, and that made him more dangerous than ever. He was angered by the disappointing outcome of the previous season when the return from his 18-month retirement ended with a second-round playoff loss to Orlando and whispers that he was no longer the best player in the game.

"Everyone's looking for just one little slip-up so they can create a big hole in my game," Jordan said during the Bulls' championship drive. "When I came back last year, I created a big hole, and I worked all summer to close that hole. I have to make sure no holes evolve in my game.

"People will say, 'Oh, Pippen's the best player on this team,' or 'Penny Hardaway's the best player in the East' or 'Hakeem Olajuwon or Shaq are the best players in the game.'" Well, I stopped all that conversation. The bottom line is, while I'm still on the court, don't try to move anyone into my spot. I'm the only one who will decide that. Only me."

And, as far as Michael was concerned, when comparing champions, there was a concrete way to settle the discussion.

Seventy-two and ten.

# HOW SW

## GOLDEN STATE 4, WASHINGTON 0

| MAY 18 | GOLDEN STATE | 101 | AT | WASHINGTON | 95 |
| MAY 20 | WASHINGTON | 91 | AT | GOLDEN STATE | 92 |
| MAY 23 | WASHINGTON | 101 | AT | GOLDEN STATE | 109 |
| MAY 25 | GOLDEN STATE | 96 | AT | WASHINGTON | 95 |

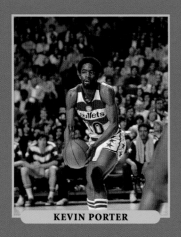

KEVIN PORTER

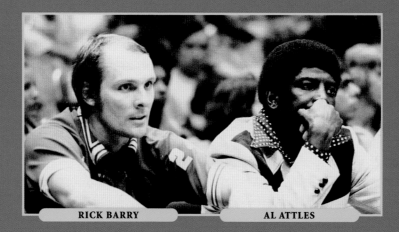

RICK BARRY

AL ATTLES

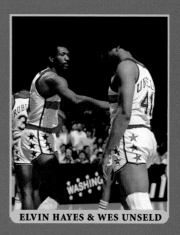

ELVIN HAYES & WES UNSELD

## WARRIORS UPSET BULLETS

Maybe it was because the country's revolutionary spirit had shifted away from the deadly serious issues of the '60s (race and war), but by the time the '70s rolled around, America was actually beginning to accept, if not grow comfortable with, the once-radical notion of change. Even on our playing fields, the difference was palpable. The hair grew longer, the uniforms became louder, and players — our burgeoning millionaire class — became more flamboyant.

Perhaps that explains how the 1975 NBA Finals failed to stir any grand revolutionary passions. When the Washington Bullets and Golden State Warriors met for Game 1 of this best-of-seven championship series at the Capital Centre in Landover, Md., hardly any attention was given to the fact that the two head

coaches — Washington's K.C. Jones and the Warriors' Al Attles — were black.

Even to this day, few who recall the Warriors' upset of the Bullets remember that the '75 Finals marked the first time in mainstream American professional sports history where the two coaches in a championship contest were African-American.

Maybe it was because Bill Russell, as a player-coach, had already led the Boston Celtics to back-to-back titles in '68 and '69. Or maybe it was because with Lenny Wilkens coaching in Portland, along with Jones and Attles, African-Americans were no longer a rarity on NBA sidelines.

Maybe it was because not enough people were captivated by the Finals because the NBA of 1975 was not the made-for-prime-

# EEP IT IS!

## WARRIORS WIN IN FOUR

By Art Spander

For the Warriors, it was the realization of the Great American Dream. For the Washington Bullets it was yet another nightmare.

Taking over the ...

over Buffalo and Boston in the preliminary rounds, was so heavily favored in the finals it wasn't a question of who but how many.

The Bullets were 3-1 choices of the odds-makers and in the minds of some very knowledgeable people, like general managers and coaches, the thinking was it might not go four games.

"... of course. The Warriors had been beating the opposition—all year. And when they got even when everything was going ... all end up right. And, for the ...

... who gets off comm...

Warriors coach Al Attles, trying to protect his top man, Rick Barry, after Barry was karate-chopped by Washington's Mike Riordan 3½ minutes into the game, was ejected and given two technical fouls.

"We looked over at the bench," said 11-year guard Jeff Mullins, "and we didn't have that reassuring person to turn to. I thought that might be a problem."

But Joe Roberts, the Warriors' assistant, took control of the bench—and the ... then the Warriors, who fell behind ... the second quarter, ... the ... aways.

said Barry, who in the final game of his most marvelous season picked up 20 points and the Sport magazine award as the playoff MVP. "They said we would lose. But the Bullets were the ones who folded. For a team eight points up, they looked like they were behind. The pressure was getting to them. The more pressure we applied the more tired they got. You could see it in their e...

And, shortly, it was manifest...

Keith Wilkes, who agai... excellent job defending H... left to cut the defi...

> "It has to be the greatest upset in the history of the NBA Finals. *Sports Illustrated* didn't even do a cover story on us. They didn't expect us to win. But few people paid any attention to it."
>
> RICK BARRY

time television event it is today. Or perhaps more importantly, it was because few people expected the Warriors to knock off the heavily favored Bullets.

Yet the Warriors not only pulled off the huge upset, they became only the third NBA team to sweep a championship series, humiliating the Bullets in four consecutive games. Led by All-Stars Elvin Hayes, Wes Unseld and Phil Chenier, the Bullets had tied Boston for the league's best record at 60-22 and defeated the Celtics in the Eastern Conference Finals, four games to two.

The Warriors won the Pacific Division with a 48-34 mark and led by the league's second-leading scorer, Rick Barry (30.6 points per game), seemed to be mostly a gang of overachievers.

The first two games of the series should have been played in Landover, Md., but because of a scheduling quirk, the Bullets played only one game at home before traveling to Golden State for the next two. After losing the first game 101-95, the pressure mounted on the Bullets players. Then came two more narrow defeats on the road — 92-91 and 109-101 — when an unstoppable Barry scored 36 and 38 points, respectively. The pressure was enormous by the time the series returned to Landover for the fourth game. But it was too late. The Warriors had the confidence; the Bullets had doubts, and the result was a scintillating one-point victory for the Warriors, 96-95, with Butch Beard clinching it with a pair of free throws with nine seconds left.

"It has to be the greatest upset in the history of the NBA Finals," said Barry. "*Sports Illustrated* didn't even do a cover story on us. They didn't expect us to win. But few people paid any attention to it."

# BIRD OF

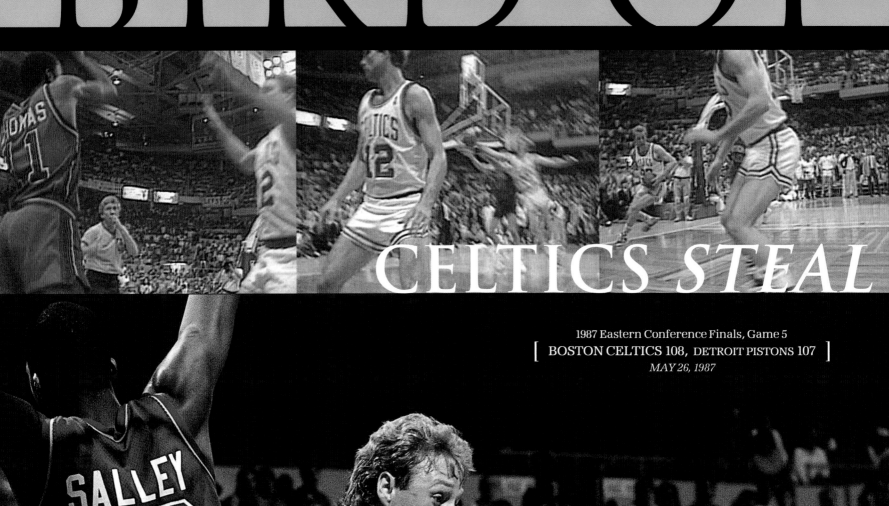

# CELTICS *STEAL*

1987 Eastern Conference Finals, Game 5

[ BOSTON CELTICS 108,  DETROIT PISTONS 107 ]

*MAY 26, 1987*

# PREY

< CAMERA ONE >

## ONE FROM THE PISTONS

< CAMERA TWO >

From the view of the winner, a great moment in time is a delightful blur of joy. But what can we cull from the observations of the man on the *wrong* side of that moment? What does it say about a man who in one devastating moment seems to be utterly crushed by defeat, yet ultimately becomes inspired by it?

cutthroat destroyers. If you let up even the slightest bit, he would find a way to win. And so it was on this day. With four seconds remaining and the Celtics trailing by one point, Bird stole an inbounds pass from Thomas and dished it off to Dennis Johnson, who cut to the basket and sank a layup. One second was left when Boston secured the victory, and Boston Garden

you let them down …" Thomas said, shaking his head.

"When your confidence is shaken," he concluded, "theirs is shattered."

Some men are crushed by defeat. The great ones, like Thomas, are galvanized by it. He used the gut-wrenching moment as motivation to try to push the Pistons past Boston and become the elite team in the

*As his Celtic teammates raced up to Bird to hug him, Thomas stood frozen in defeat.*

In the final moments of Game 5 of the 1987 NBA Eastern Conference Finals, we learned a great deal about two of pro basketball's most remarkable winners — Boston's Larry Bird and Detroit's Isiah Thomas. In the blink of an eye, in the final seconds of a shocking 108-107 Celtics triumph, Bird snatched certain victory from Thomas' hands.

Bird was one of the game's ultimate

turned into a mad house.

As his Celtic teammates raced up to Bird to hug him, Thomas stood frozen in defeat. He had wanted the ball in his hands in moments like this, and dreamed of joining Bird and Magic Johnson on that narrow pedestal as his generation's most reliable winners. "When you're the leader, and everyone is giving you their trust and confidence and they believe in you, and

East. And it worked. The following season, the Pistons knocked off the Celtics in the playoffs, made three straight trips to the NBA Finals and became only the third team in league history to win back-to-back NBA titles with victories in 1989 and 1990. They could not have done it without Thomas, who became the role model as a player who learned from his mistakes, and grew to illustrious heights.

# THE 1980
# DECLARATION
## *of*
# MAGIC

*His basketball charms had mesmerized a legion of fans
long before he officially became an icon at age 20.
In the previous three seasons, Earvin "Magic" Johnson had won
a Michigan high school championship, an NCAA title at
Michigan State, and in Game 6 of the 1980 NBA Finals, he
was one step away from adding a professional championship.*

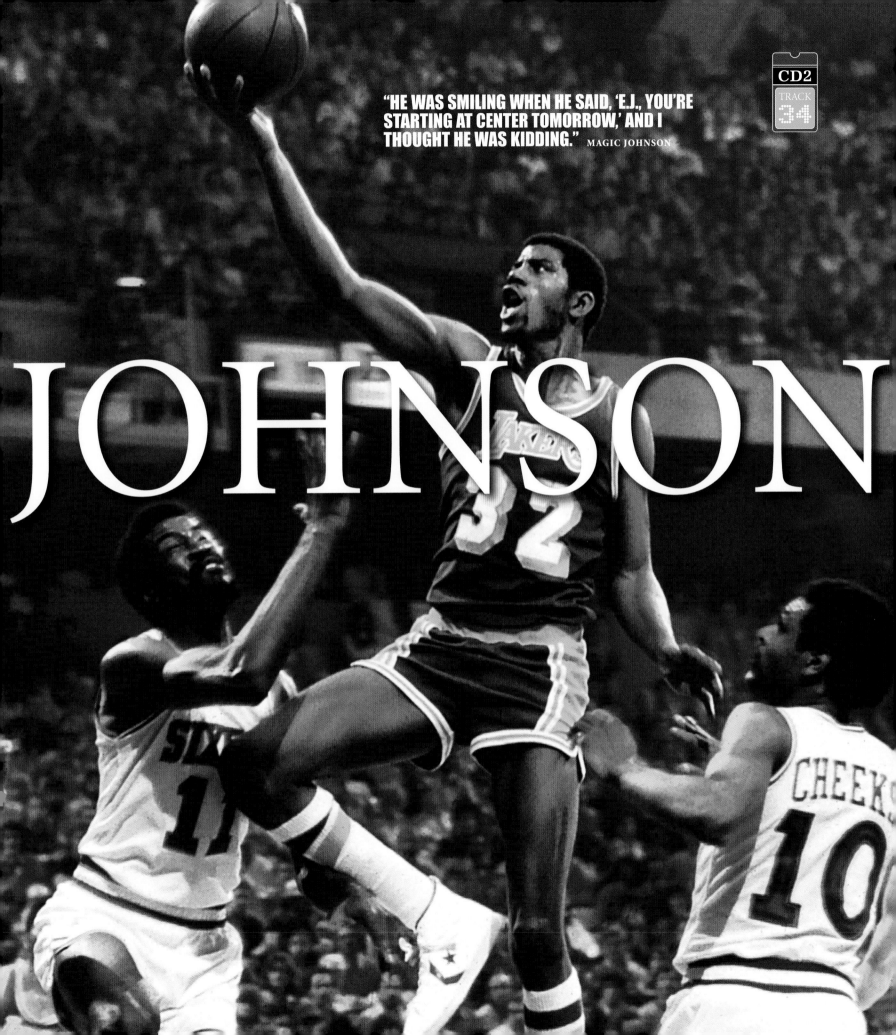

"HE WAS SMILING WHEN HE SAID, 'E.J., YOU'RE STARTING AT CENTER TOMORROW,' AND I THOUGHT HE WAS KIDDING." MAGIC JOHNSON

JOHNSON

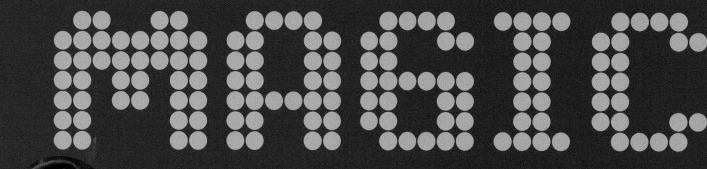

# MAGIC

## "... still today my greatest game in the NBA."
**MAGIC JOHNSON**

It was a tall order, even for a 6-foot-9 point guard because Johnson and the Los Angeles Lakers would meet the Philadelphia 76ers without the benefit of having Kareem Abdul-Jabbar, who ultimately became the leading scorer in NBA history. **Johnson had a dazzling, megawatt smile, a flashy game rooted on unselfishness, and leadership ability unmatched by any star of his stature in NBA history.** On the night of Game 6, he was on pro basketball's biggest stage at the end of his rookie year after only two years in college, and all he was required to do was hoist a veteran-ladened Lakers team on his youthful shoulders.

Los Angeles had a 3-2 lead in the best-of-seven series over Julius Erving's 76ers, but Abdul-Jabbar was at home, unable to walk because of an ankle sprain. **Johnson was asked to do the unthinkable, shifting from point guard to the pivot, where he was so inexperienced that he had to practice the position of his feet before the center jump to start that game.**

By the end of the game, it was evident that nothing on the basketball court was foreign to the Magic Man, who put on an incredible performance by scoring 42 points, grabbing 15 rebounds, handing out seven assists and even tossing in three

steals for good measure. The Kareem-less Lakers stunned Philly, 123-107 to clinch the first of Johnson's five NBA titles.

"We got the news that Kareem was not going to play and we were all in shock," Johnson recalled two decades later. "It's like, 'Man, I can't believe he's actually not going to play.'"

Johnson knew that he had to step up his on-court performance in order for the Lakers to win, and he was equipped to do exactly that. Because of his joyous smile, one facet of Johnson's personality had not been noticed by many, including some on his team. **Beneath that giddy, energetic persona lay the heart of a ferocious competitor, a totalitarian when there was an opportunity for victory. So when the Lakers boarded the team plane and his teammates saw Abdul-Jabbar's empty seat at the front of the cabin, Magic plopped down in the seat and winked at his teammates, "Never fear, E.J. is here."**

"And they all looked at me like I'm silly," Johnson said. "It was like, 'This young kid ... yeaaaah, right.'"

Waiting for their flight to Philadelphia, Coach Paul Westhead had already told Johnson that he'd jump center against Caldwell Jones.

"He was smiling when he said, 'E.J.,

you're starting at center tomorrow,' and I thought he was kidding," Johnson said.

With Magic pushing the fast break relentlessly, the Lakers plan was to run the bigger, less athletic 76ers into the ground. **By halftime, the up-tempo game plan was working, with the score tied at 60-all. Then came the second-half explosion. A 14-0 run opened the third quarter for Los Angeles, and the soldout Spectrum crowd was silenced.**

"They couldn't believe what was happening," said Johnson.

Lost in Magic's brilliant moment was the play of Jamaal Wilkes, the forward who was so smooth that he was called Silk. Wilkes finished with 37 points and 10 rebounds, including 25 points in the second half. "Jamaal had the greatest hands," said Magic. "I'd never have any doubt when I let one go. He'd catch it. He was a great big-game player. Silk was on, just like I knew he would be."

But history remembers this more as a Magical moment, which Johnson continues to call "still today my greatest game in the NBA."

So great, in fact, that Johnson can't get enough of it. He had a VCR tape of the game but played it so much that the tape burned up, a condition the Sixers could understand.

## 42 pts 15 rbs 7 assts 3 stls

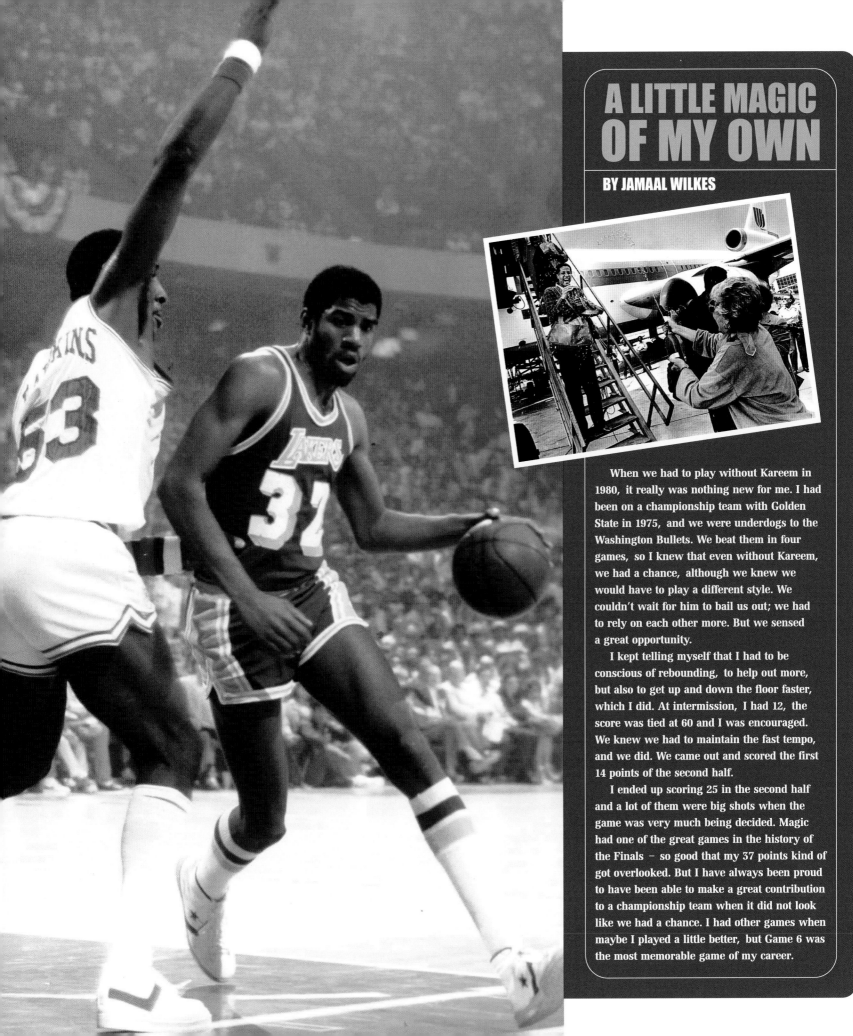

# A LITTLE MAGIC OF MY OWN

**BY JAMAAL WILKES**

When we had to play without Kareem in 1980, it really was nothing new for me. I had been on a championship team with Golden State in 1975, and we were underdogs to the Washington Bullets. We beat them in four games, so I knew that even without Kareem, we had a chance, although we knew we would have to play a different style. We couldn't wait for him to bail us out; we had to rely on each other more. But we sensed a great opportunity.

I kept telling myself that I had to be conscious of rebounding, to help out more, but also to get up and down the floor faster, which I did. At intermission, I had 12, the score was tied at 60 and I was encouraged. We knew we had to maintain the fast tempo, and we did. We came out and scored the first 14 points of the second half.

I ended up scoring 25 in the second half and a lot of them were big shots when the game was very much being decided. Magic had one of the great games in the history of the Finals — so good that my 37 points kind of got overlooked. But I have always been proud to have been able to make a great contribution to a championship team when it did not look like we had a chance. I had other games when maybe I played a little better, but Game 6 was the most memorable game of my career.

# DISHING
## THE ROCK

**CD2**
**TRACK 35**

**ORLANDO MAGIC 155,
DENVER NUGGETS 116
DECEMBER 30, 1990**

## SKILES
### SIZZLES WITH
# 30
## ASSISTS

*Out of all the point guards in NBA history, the idea that Scott Skiles would become the record holder for most assists in a game is as unlikely as a house painter ending up in the Louvre.*

Skiles was a scrappy, rough-edged journeyman who bounced around among five teams in a 10-year career. He lacked the stylish, misdirection wizardry of Magic Johnson and Bob Cousy. He had none of the jitterbugging, open-court flair of Isiah Thomas, Nate Archibald or Kevin Porter. These guys were artists. Skiles was a lunch-pail-toting laborer. But whatever he lacked in style, Skiles made up for in effort, and on December 30, 1990, while playing for the Orlando Magic, his efforts were rewarded with an NBA record 30 assists in a 155-116 rout of the Denver Nuggets.

### "I knew that I had quite a few of them," Skiles said after breaking Porter's 12-year-old mark of 29 set while playing for the New Jersey Nets.

The best way to describe Skiles' playing style was quite simple: by any means necessary.

He wasn't flashy, just effective. He would find any conceivable way to get the ball in his teammates' hands. Many of Skiles' assists on that night against the Nuggets came when he was knocked to the floor scrambling for a loose ball. He looked like a rugby player in a scrum, burrowing through a tangle of arms and legs, then somehow bouncing a pass from the pile to a teammate flashing to the hoop.

Yet with six minutes to go in the game, it didn't appear that Skiles would ever break the record. He had tied Porter's mark at that point, and began feeding teammate Jerry Reynolds for wide-open jumpers. But Reynolds was oblivious, and would drive to the hoop, eliminating the possibility of an assist.

Finally, with only 19.6 seconds left, Reynolds caught on. Skiles gave him a pass on the left wing and he popped in a 22-footer to give Skiles the record. The sellout crowd of 15,077 at Orlando Arena gave the future head coach of the Phoenix Suns a standing ovation, an appropriate response since they had just seen a masterpiece.

# LENNY PASSES A LEGEND
## Wilkens Overtakes Auerbach as Winningest Coach

[ ATLANTA HAWKS 112, WASHINGTON BULLETS 90 ]
*JANUARY 6, 1995*

As the streamers and confetti came down from the rafters, and Lenny Wilkens had at long last caught Red Auerbach for most coaching victories in NBA history, the 57-year-old basketball lifer came up with the perfect tribute to the living legend he was passing.

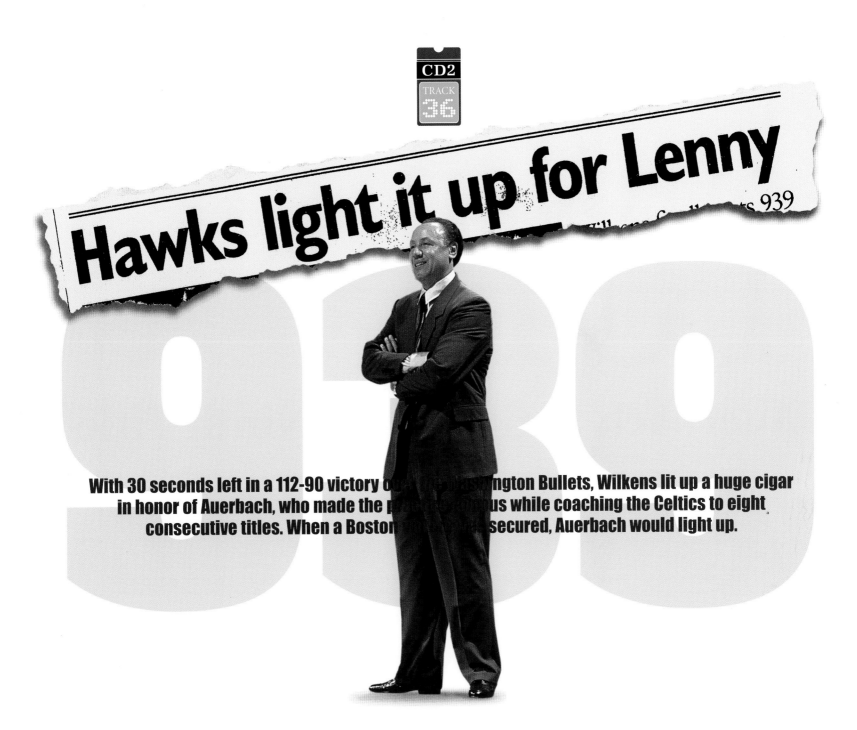

# Hawks light it up for Lenny

**With 30 seconds left in a 112-90 victory over the Washington Bullets, Wilkens lit up a huge cigar in honor of Auerbach, who made the practice famous while coaching the Celtics to eight consecutive titles. When a Boston victory was secured, Auerbach would light up.**

he journey to the top of the all-time victory list began in 1969 when Wilkens, a nine-time All-Star, was named player-coach of the Seattle SuperSonics. Twenty-five years and three teams later, Wilkens earned victory No. 938 on December 29, 1994. Yet the record-breaker would not come so easily. In his book *Unguarded: My Forty Years Surviving in the NBA*, Wilkens recalled the pressure his players were under as he closed in on the record-breaking victory:

**"I tied Red's record on December 29 … one more victory, that's all we needed. The next night we played in Cleveland, where it would have been nice to set the record. The Hawks management packed several caps with the number 939 to bring with us, along with a victory cake. We lost by two points."**

According to Wilkens, when the Hawks traveled back home to play Portland, the caps and cake came along for the ride. The Hawks lost again. This pattern repeated itself when Atlanta traveled to New York. Caps, cake. Another loss.

**"On the flight home," said Wilkens, "We all just ate the cake before it turned stale."**

Wilkens, who along with John Wooden are the only men in the Naismith Memorial Basketball Hall of Fame as both coach and player, believed his team was distracted by the commotion over the run to the record. But finally, a week after tying Auerbach, the lowly Bullets arrived at Atlanta's Omni on January 6, 1995. The Hawks played as loose as could be, and easily won the game.

Although he paid tribute to Auerbach, Wilkens did not light up without a price. A non-smoker, Wilkens said he nearly choked while puffing on the cigar. No one ever said that becoming a legend was easy.

# OUT ON TOP:

# Auerbach Retires After Ninth Title

**A**mong basketball aficionados the image of Red Auerbach masticating on a victory cigar was as identifiable as the golden arches are now to fast food devotees. For what qualifies as a basketball epoch, the former seemed as ubiquitous as the latter is today. Auerbach's victory cigars had a dual purpose. He was celebrating victory while also sending a message of Celtics superiority to enraged opponents, who sometimes had to watch Auerbach light up in the third quarter with the Celts up by 30.

**THE BOSTON SUNDAY HERALD SPORTS SECTION**

SUNDAY, APRIL 14, 1957 — PAGE FIFTY-SEVEN

Heinsohn Leads Way with 37 Points; Russell Also Excels

# CELTICS TAKE TITLE, 125

A jubilant Red Auerbach celebrates another NBA championship with the Boston Garden faithful.

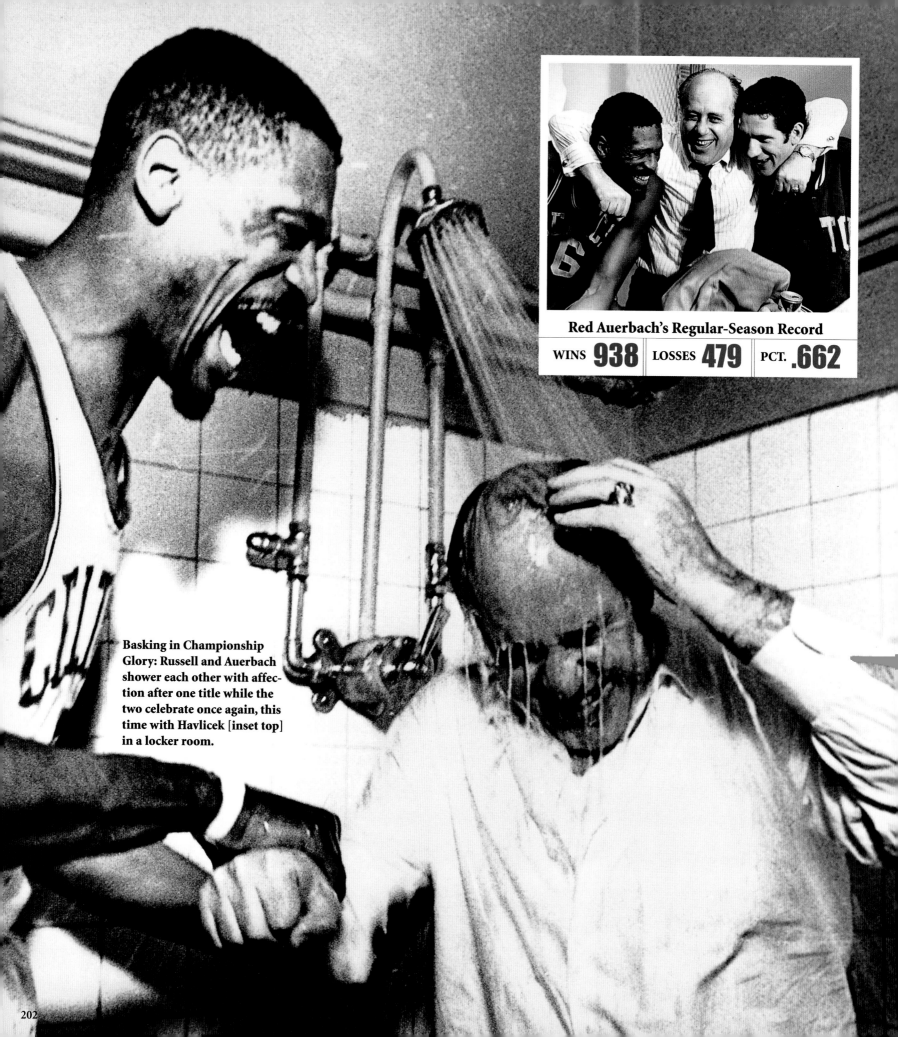

**Red Auerbach's Regular-Season Record**

| WINS | | LOSSES | | PCT. | |
|---|---|---|---|---|---|
| | **938** | | **479** | | **.662** |

**Basking in Championship Glory: Russell and Auerbach shower each other with affection after one title while the two celebrate once again, this time with Havlicek [inset top] in a locker room.**

*But, as Muhammad Ali once said, "If you can do it, it ain't bragging." And that was the case with Auerbach, who guided the Boston Celtics to nine titles in 10 years, including eight consecutive championships from 1959-66.*

*"You have to say the first one is always the biggest," said Auerbach. "That one came against St. Louis when the seventh game went into double-overtime. But the last one was great too."*

*1957 World Champions*

In winning that last title in 1966, Auerbach was at his best. The Celtics were an aging group and for the first time in a decade they didn't win the Eastern Division, finishing a game behind Philadelphia. Boston defeated Cincinnati in the opening round and, after losing six of 10 games to Philadelphia and Wilt Chamberlain in the regular season, dispensed of the Sixers 4-1 in the Eastern finals.

Standing in the Celtics' way were the Los Angeles Lakers. Boston had faced the Lakers in three of the previous four Finals, with the Celtics winning each time, but the Lakers opened on a positive note, capturing the first game in overtime 133-129.

Auerbach, however, was one of the great showmen and master manipulators in NBA history. He countered the Lakers' victory with a bombshell. Auerbach, who had already declared his intention to retire as coach following the season, announced after Game 1 that Bill Russell would succeed him.

The Celtics won the next three games and went on to win the title, four games to three. "It was a great way to go out," Auerbach said.

"They pulled a fast one, announcing that Russell was taking over," Gail Goodrich said. "We won Game 1, but it was buried under the announcement. Red was saving it just for when it would work against us the most."

But that was Auerbach, whose ninth and final championship as a coach may have been his best.

1957

1959

1960

1961

1962

1963

1964

1965

1966

Celtic Championships Under Red Auerbach

McNichols Arena, Denver
[ DETROIT PISTONS 186, DENVER NUGGETS 184, 3 OT ]
*DECEMBER 13, 1983*

CHUCK DALY

DOUG MOE

# MILE HIGH SCORE

DETROIT

DENVER

CD2
TRACK
38

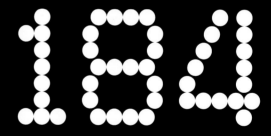

*It was supposed to be a routine game, one of 82 for the Denver Nuggets and the Detroit Pistons, two teams without championship aspirations, but intent on competing and putting on a good show for the Nuggets fans. And they usually did because one trait the Pistons and Nuggets had in common was: They were much better on offense than they were on defense.*

"You couldn't write a book with a better script. After this game, both teams deserve a week off. It seems like we played three games tonight. It's the greatest game I've ever played in or seen."

KELLY TRIPUCKA

The Denver Post Thursday, Dec. 15, 1983

NUGGETS/NBA
Detroit, Denver expect to score a lot, but . . .

Pistons win a 'nuke-out'

| | 1 | 2 | 3 | 4 | 1OT | 2OT | 3OT | Tot |
|---|---|---|---|---|---|---|---|---|
| Detroit | 38 | 36 | 34 | 37 | 14 | 12 | 15 | 186 |
| Denver | 34 | 40 | 39 | 32 | 14 | 12 | 13 | 184 |

# "FIRST ONE TO 140 WINS."

**CHUCK DALY**

The 1983-84 season was a couple of months old and Detroit was 10-12, winding up a West Coast road trip with the stop in Denver. The Nuggets had an 11-11 record. Both Detroit papers did not deem the game worthy enough to pay for travel costs for a staff writer, and one Denver paper gave its beat writer the night off and covered the game with a backup.

Here's what they missed:

**Three overtimes, four players scoring more than 40 points each, the teams combining for 142 field goals, 370 combined points and a 186-184 Detroit victory, which set a record for the highest scoring games by a winning and losing team.**

"One word — unbelievable," said Detroit's Kelly Tripucka, who finished with 35 points. "You couldn't write a book with a better script. After this game, both teams deserve a week off. It seems like we played three games tonight. It's the greatest game I've ever played in or seen."

Nothing seemed to stem the flood of baskets by each side on that cold Denver night. Defense was pure matador. The scoreboard lit up like a pinball machine.

"First one to 140 wins," first-year Detroit coach Chuck Daly had joked with his Denver counterpart Doug Moe when their paths crossed just before tipoff. And the score at the end of the first quarter — Detroit 38, Denver 34 — made Daly appear clairvoyant.

**KIKI VANDEWEGHE**

At halftime the score was tied at 74 and there was no doubt that the game had turned into a run-and-gun, high-light-film slugfest. After three quarters, the Nuggets had pulled ahead, 113-108. And still there were 12 minutes to go in regulation.

Stuck in the middle of all this scoring and the culprit in sending the game into its first overtime was a whirling dervish named Isiah Thomas, who would score a career-high 47 points. Denver was up by two, 145-143, when Thomas — at 6-foot-1, the smallest man on the floor — slithered between all the other bodies, grabbed a missed Bill Laimbeer free throw and put it back to send the game into overtime.

Dan Issel had a chance to win it for Denver in the final seconds of the first overtime, but a jumper from the top of the key missed. The score was knotted at 159. Tripucka single-handedly kept the Pistons in the game then, scoring all 12 of Detroit's points over the next five minutes, to send it to a third overtime tied at 171.

**After more than three hours, and all of those points, the Pistons finally found the strength, in the game's final seconds, to play enough defense to shut down the Nuggets. Thomas got a steal and Laimbeer made a block, and both teams wobbled to their locker rooms.**

"It was a really tough loss to take," Moe said. "I thought we played pretty well, but they were great."

**The Pistons and Nuggets broke six NBA records that night:**

| Most points by two teams | Most points by one team | Most field goals made by two teams | Most assists by two teams |
| --- | --- | --- | --- |
| 370 | 186 | 142 | 93 |

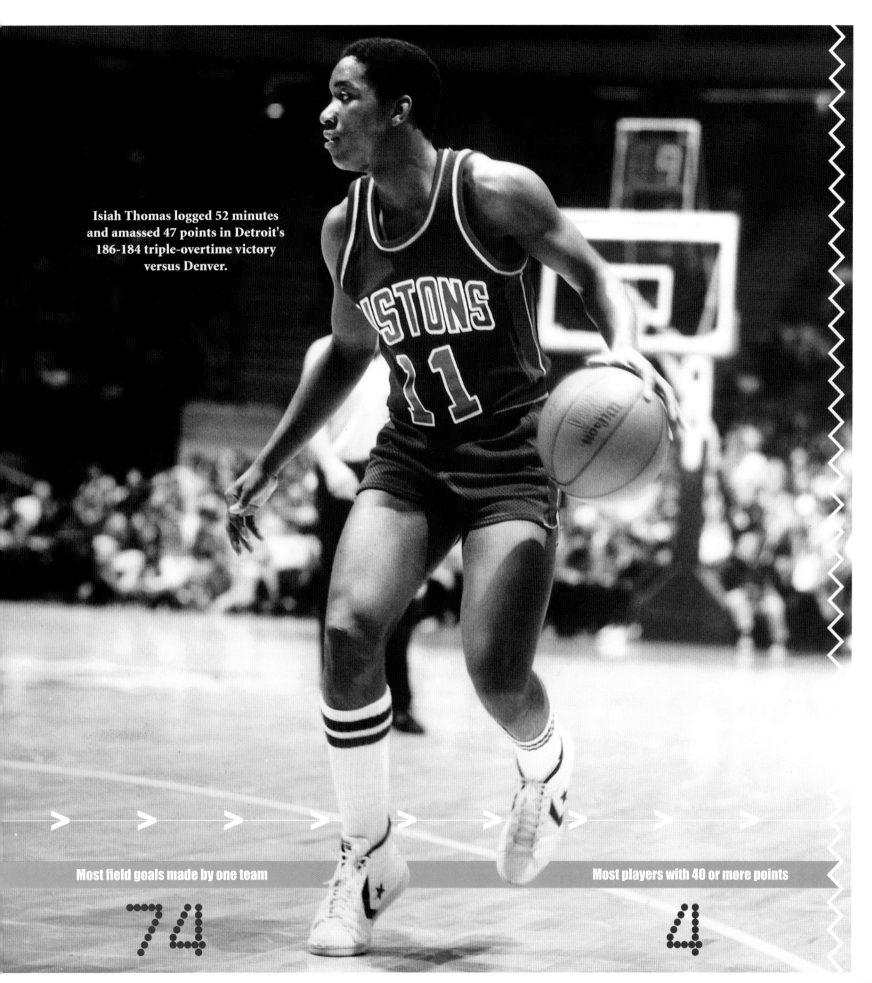

Isiah Thomas logged 52 minutes and amassed 47 points in Detroit's 186-184 triple-overtime victory versus Denver.

Most field goals made by one team

74

Most players with 40 or more points

4

# CHAPTER 9

# FINAL MOMENTS

## GOODBYE MOMENTS FOR THE GREAT ONES

When the NBA's transcendent stars come face to face with their athletic mortality
and decide the time has come to walk away, the public that has embraced them for so long
and with such enthusiasm is reluctant to let go. Many times, it is almost as if fans and teammates must
do something elaborate, not only to pay homage to the stars,
but also to reconcile the loss for themselves. Kareem Abdul-Jabbar and Larry Bird were among many
of the great ones whose send-offs were as unique as their games.

After playing 20 seasons and logging over 66,000 regular-season and playoff minutes, it was fitting that
while President George Bush and legendary announcer Chick Hearn feted Abdul-Jabbar in front of 17,505 adoring
fans in the Forum on April 23, 1989, the Lakers' captain sat in an oversized rocking chair and smiled.

**"I never knew how people felt about me," Abdul-Jabbar said.
"I never realized some of these people appreciated what I did in my career."**

When the Boston faithful bid adieu to Bird on February 4, 1993, it was its own event, with no game to follow.
Yet, more than 15,000 showed up as No. 33 was hoisted to the Garden rafters.

**"Larry, you only told me one lie,"** said rival and friend Magic Johnson, who teamed with Bird
in the early '80s to usher in the league's Golden Era. **"You said there will be another Larry Bird.
Larry, there will never, ever be another Larry Bird."**

Departing superstars demonstrate why cliches ring so true in the sports world —
because they may be gone, but they will never be forgotten.

### OTHER CHAPTER 9 MOMENTS

Magic in the Land of Disney
A Storybook All-Star Ending

# MAGIC

**CD2** TRACK **48**

## IN THE LAND OF DISNEY:

### A STORYBOOK ALL-STAR ENDING

Among the Eastern All-Stars who embraced Magic's return to the hardwood were Detroit's Joe Dumars and Cleveland's Mark Price.

Orlando Arena, Orlando

## [ WEST ALL-STARS 153, EAST ALL-STARS 113 ]

*FEBRUARY 9, 1992*

The electricity increased with each introduction. A moment like no other in NBA history was at hand, and everyone fortunate enough to be in the Orlando Arena knew it.

The date was February 9, 1992. Lineups for the 42nd NBA All-Star Game were being introduced. Twelve players from the East, the first team to take the floor, were standing at one free throw line while their 12 counterparts from the West were greeted by warm applause from a sellout crowd of 14,272.

**The first sign that it would be a remarkable day occurred when the warm applause suddenly turned to cheers, then built to a collective roar, and ultimately to a deafening blast. On this day, the West had a 13th All-Star, a man who had dazzled a generation and jump-started a league: Magic Johnson.**

Only three months after announcing his retirement because he had contracted the human immunodeficiency virus (HIV), the virus that causes AIDS, Johnson returned an All-Star and basketball protocol were tossed aside. Consider the beginning: After Johnson was introduced, good friend Isiah Thomas led the East stars across the court to a surprised Johnson. One by one they embraced him, and Johnson never stopped smiling.

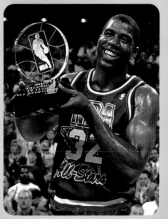

"I think he was shocked," Thomas said.

"Words mean a lot," Johnson said, "but it's feelings that count most. Ours is a game of compassion. I'll never forget those hugs and high-fives."

**Consider the end: With 14.5 seconds left in the game, Johnson lofted a three-point shot as he was falling backward. Nothing but net. It was so appropriate, so absolutely perfect that the players simply quit playing at that point. Everyone ran up to Johnson and embraced him again.**

"It was the first game ever called on account of hugs," Johnson fondly recalled later.

Johnson, who had not played during the 1991-92 season, ended the day with 25 points and the Most Valuable Player trophy. Five months later, he would be on the gold medal-winning Dream Team at the Barcelona Olympics. He would return briefly to play for the Lakers during the 1995-96 season, but only to bring proper closure to his career.

Devoted hoops fans, however, prefer to remember the way Magic brought closure to his All-Star career.

"It was storybook," West coach Don Nelson said. "It was pure Disney."

# AFTERWORD

## BY KARL MALONE

When you make a great play on the basketball court and it becomes part of NBA history, you cherish it, take pride in it and you never forget it. It has a special place in your heart and soul.

During my 16 years in the NBA, I have been fortunate to have experienced many incredible moments. I've been to the NBA Finals, won Most Valuable Player awards during the regular season and All-Star Games, made a lot of all-NBA teams and even scored more points than one of the true basketball legends, Wilt Chamberlain. The memories will be with me for the rest of my life.

**I love the excitement of a big game, the feeling I get from a monster dunk and creating a moment that is celebrated by my teammates, family, friends and fans. But my definition of a great moment is probably different than it is for most players or fans, because every time I step on a basketball court, it's a great moment for me. I also feel that every time I step on the court, I have the responsibility to make it a great moment for my teammates, our coaches and everyone watching us.**

My approach has always been to improve every year and be consistent every game. Not for five games or two months, but for the whole year. A lot of people talk about raising your game for the playoffs. I say that every player should raise his level of play for every game and then go into the playoffs ready to play the exact same way he has played during the regular season. **For me, every game is a playoff game, every moment is a crucial one, and I am proud that it's been that way for my whole career.**

To make great plays, you have to get yourself ready. It's no accident that the thrilling moments you have read about in this book have been from the best players in the history of the game. Because those are the guys who put themselves in *position* to make those plays by taking care of themselves and playing hard every night.

All great players have a common approach to the game. Guys like Michael Jordan, Magic Johnson, Larry Bird, Julius Erving, Kareem Abdul-Jabbar, Wilt Chamberlain, Bill Russell, and certainly my teammate John Stockton, think the same way I do. I want my teammates and coaches to know that I want to be a professional every day of my life. I would like to think that if I had to play a game two months after the season is over — 30 minutes, 35 minutes — I could do it, because I try to keep myself in shape. I don't take things for granted. **I do believe in working out and always being in shape. I want to set an example for the younger players.** Sure, during the offseason, I'd like to be on some cruise with my wife and kids or be in my nice car with some buddies, hanging out. But, you know what I found out? I can still do all of that *and* stay in shape. I know that I can do all the hunting, fishing and camping I want, ride my motorcycle, spend time with my family, and *still* have time to train.

So great plays don't happen by accident. They are not random. **A great play is great because the player who makes it is at a level higher than the average, or even the star player. That's why they invented the term "*super*star."**

Great players want to to be great every night. One thing that has

always pushed me is that no matter how successful I am as a basketball player, I never forget what it is like to be a fan who pays good money to watch us play. Those fans go to work every day, punch the clock, work from 9-to-5 and they can't take a day off just because they don't feel good. I know a lot of people who have everyday jobs, and if they have to work with a stomach flu, a head cold, a migraine, bad knees or whatever, they still go to work. We as professional athletes get paid good money, so if I'm not feeling very well, is it fair for me not to play? Am I being fair to the fans?

Even if I do feel bad, I never tell a teammate, because all that does is give you an excuse to fail. If you tell everyone you're sick and then you don't play well, afterward people will say: "Well, Karl didn't have a good game tonight, but he wasn't feeling right." **So I'm going to play and keep quiet about whatever's bothering me. In my personal list of great moments, one that I am very proud of is that in 16 years I've missed only three games because of injuries.**

That approach is similar to the approach of a lot of players in this book. And that's why they are in this book — because they not only have the skill, but they also have the dedication that sets the stage for great moments.

As players, we know about those moments, which is why you will find a lot of us talking about Wilt. Kareem has scored more points than any player in NBA history, and I have nothing but respect for Kareem. **But I have to tell you that when I passed Wilt on the all-time list of scorers to rank second in the history of the game, I think I had the ultimate feeling. If I can continue to play and someday pass Kareem, I can't imagine it being any more special than passing Wilt.**

Because Wilt was a monument. He was an institution. He scored 100 points in a game, and all players still believe that is the greatest feat of all-time. But I think there was one accomplishment that was even bigger. One season, Wilt played every minute of every game. And because a few games went into overtime, he *averaged* 48.5 minutes a game that year. The game is only 48 minutes long!

As I said, I pride myself on playing every night and being ready to play every night. But that's one record that I can't even imagine. They say in sports that records are made to be broken, but I can guarantee you that Wilt created a record that will never be touched.

Many plays in this book will never be equaled, and that's why great moments are so special. Last-second shots, incredible moves,

all-time records, and many other moments that will never be forgotten. If you love basketball, however, *all* moments are memorable. Every second of every game. I was at a game one night last season and a fan walked up to me and said: "Wow, Karl. This is your 16th year and you're still going strong. You're going to keep scoring 30 points a night for another 10 years."

That made me laugh. Ten years might not be realistic, but the fact that someone believes I can do that is an unbelievable compliment. It means that he respects my approach to the game. It also means that when he watches me, whether it's in the first quarter of the first game of the season, or the last quarter of a playoff game, it is a special moment for him. And that means a lot to me, because when I retire, I want to be able to tell myself that I never did just show up for games, I did everything I could to make each and every moment special.

The great moments continue, right up to the present. While this book was being produced,
the Los Angeles Lakers were putting together an unprecedented 15-1 playoff record, the best in NBA history.
Does that make them the greatest team in NBA history? There is no accurate way to answer, but the 2000-01